Education for a Globalizing Asia

Education for a Globalizing Asia

*

Challenges and Opportunities

Edited by
Enrique Niño P. Leviste

ATENEO CENTER FOR ASIAN STUDIES

ATENEO CENTER FOR ASIAN STUDIES
School of Social Sciences
Loyola Schools, Ateneo de Manila University
2nd Floor, Ricardo and Dr. Rosita Leong Hall
Loyola Heights, Quezon City
P.O. Box 154, Manila 1099
Telephone: 4266001 loc. 5285

Cover design by Felix Mago Miguel
Book design by Paolo Tiausas

The National Library of the Philippines CIP Data

Recommended entry:

Education for globalizing Asia / edited by Enrique Niño P. Leviste. --
Quezon City : Ateneo Center for Asian Studies., [2019], c2019.
xvi, 104 pages ; 22.86 cm

ISBN 978-971-0426-31-7

1. Education, Higher – Asia – Congresses 2. Education and globalization – Asia – Congresses. I. Leviste, Enrique Nino P. II. Title.

378.1 LC189.85 P920190017

*

Contents

*

Acknowledgements

THIS BOOK SUSTAINS a post-conference practice that goes back to the first of the biennial international conferences of the Ateneo Center for Asian Studies (ACAS) in 2001. As the practice would have it, ACAS publishes a selection of papers and commentaries presented in the conference as a way of extending its contribution to knowledge about Asia. The present work is derived from the eighth conference held in 2016 on the theme "Education for a Globalizing Asia: Challenges and Opportunities," and therefore acknowledgement is due to colleagues and friends who helped organize the conference as much as to those who saw to the book's publication.

We thank Dr. Enrique Niño P. Leviste for serving as the book's editor, and providing invaluable advice in the selection of resource persons for the conference; the members of the ACAS board of directors—Dr. Manuel Dy, Dr. Ellen Palanca, Dr. Ruben Mendoza, Dr. Diana Mendoza, and Dr. Anne Candelaria—for reviewing the abstracts submitted to the conference, and for further screening them for publication in this book; Dr. Cornelia Soto and Dr. Rhodora Nicdao of the Ateneo Department of Education for helping in the review; and the following Ateneo units and partners who supported the conference through financial grants and other services—the Ricardo Leong Center for Chinese Studies, the Indonesian Embassy in Manila, Confucius Center at the Ateneo de Manila University, and the Ateneo Loyola Schools Office of Internationalization.

We are enormously grateful to Dr. Fernando Aldaba, dean of the School of Social Sciences, for his support of the project, and Ramon C. Sunico of the Department of English for his guidance during all the stages of the book's preparation and for editing the manuscripts.

Violet B. Valdez
Executive Director

*

Enrique Niño P. Leviste

Introduction

THE PAPERS AND COMMENTARIES in this volume were selected from those presented at the Eighth International Conference on Asian Studies convened by the Ateneo Center for Asian Studies (ACAS) on 26 August 2016 with the theme, "Education for a Globalizing Asia: Challenges and Opportunities." These papers examined the varying effects on education systems in Asia of the adoption of strategies influenced by dominant Western paradigms in internationalizing academic institutions with the intention to make them more globally competitive. Issues confronted by these institutions as they continue to implement curricular, organizational, and procedural reforms in the name of internationalization were also afforded attention.

Education policy experts Qiang and Mok have extensively written about ongoing debates over the definition, rationale, and impact of globalization on education in Asia. They observed that the growing propensity of Asian higher education institutions to endorse and apply Western models of education reform, an apparent offshoot of the intensifying demand for globally competitive schools, has been at the core of these exchanges. They argued that the drive to internationalize, a customary response to this demand, merited a critical look because of its immense implications most notably on education governance, curriculum development and pedagogy, and organization restructuring. Qiang (2003), for instance, discussed two main arguments that justify strong support for internationalization. First, the need to prepare graduates for the demands of a global economy and labor market necessitated changes in academic and professional requirements.

Academic aptitude remains important, observed Qiang, but multilingualism, and social and intercultural skills and attitudes are also paramount. Second, internationalization raises the level of research and the size of investment in it, and ensures that avenues for collaboration and international cooperation are in place.

Mok shared a similar observation in "Questing for Internationalization of Universities in Asia: Critical Reflections" (2007). He contended that globalization and the concomitant rise of the knowledge economy led to the restructuring of higher education in the Asian region. Restructuring in universities, argued Mok, mainly entailed the application of new governance models intended to bolster global competitiveness. Global competitiveness was customarily measured in terms of increased student mobility and staff mobility, diversification of course offerings, cutting-edge research and innovative pedagogical approaches, and the establishment of infrastructures and mechanisms that promoted collaboration among academics of diverse persuasions and research interests. While Mok maintained that internationalization was not a new phenomenon, the intensity and extent of internationalization activities taking place in contemporary universities warranted closer investigation. Unlike Qiang, however, he focused on the range of dimensions and processes constituting the internationalization of education and cautioned against oversimplifications. What necessitated further understanding, maintained Mok, were multiple interpretations of internationalization reflected in specific strategies that Asian universities pursued.

Mok's comprehensive critique of international benchmarking further distinguished his work from that of Qiang's. He observed that the quest for global competitiveness, while commendable, engendered an overreliance on performance yardsticks greatly informed by Western notions of academic excellence. Such dependence made Asian universities prone to policy copying rather than policy learning. Restructuring efforts patterned after those in the West only produced more paperwork and administration instead of cultivating enabling environments for teaching, learning, and research to flourish. The fetish for global competitiveness further led to the erosion of academic freedom as education became increasingly commodified and marketized. For instance, Mok argued that the desire among academics in Asia—much like their Western counterparts—to continually publish in reputable international journals to bolster all at once university rankings and personal stature was an offshoot of the marketization and commodification of education. The sociologist Randall Collins (2002), by the same token, lamented this development in a paper on the role of universities in promoting credential inflation.

More broadly, Mok saw the strong connection between internationalization and the continuing legacy of colonialism in education. In contending that adherence to global standards and norms of competitiveness fostered a new imperialism in education, he shed light on how the perspectives and practices of the dominant metropolitan center—the US hegemony in this case—has permeated education systems in Asia in an enduring manner. The ascendancy (not to mention preponderance) of these perspectives and practices were legitimized via education reforms that became popular and mandatory in the name of academic excellence and global competitiveness. Furthermore, the implementation of these strategies, observed Mok, reinforced existing inequalities in the academe, as schools that have long been bereft of resources and administrative capacity to institute reforms experienced further marginalization.

The ACAS Eighth International Conference delved into the effects and consequences of internationalization on schools in Asia, and documented organizational, curricular, and pedagogical responses to evolving academic landscapes by focusing on specific cases. The papers selected for publication here covered a wide range of topics, from diverse perspectives on global citizenship education in three Asian countries, to an examination of the impact of globalization and deregulation on the quality of education, and an ethnographic account of the challenges confronted by two higher education institutions in building sustainable channels for research collaboration and mentoring.

While the impact of globalization on education systems emerged as the overarching theme, the papers can be further categorized into three sub-topics: internationalization initiatives and approaches to globalization in education across Asia (Alviar-Martin and Baildon, Ispandriarno and Loffelholz); experiences of internationalization at the margins (Lorenzana and Rodriguez, Guevarra); and the challenges of adhering to Western paradigms of internationalization (Nebres, Arao).

Alviar-Martin and Baildon identified two factors that hindered the institutionalization of issues-centered global citizenship education (GCE). For one, they viewed as inimical the adoption of neoliberal frameworks of reform that endorsed as urgent standards-based restructuring, high-stake examinations and ranking, international comparisons, and discourses narrowly focused on excellence. They argued that it further engendered a brand of civic education that disenfranchised and alienated young citizens. Alviar-Martin and Baildon also observed how attempts to forge a shared national identity by invoking logics of national security have been unsuccessful. Such attempts fell short in countering or were instrumental in amplifying adverse effects of entrenched political and social hierarchies. Using case studies from Singapore, Bhutan, and Japan, they noted how a depoliticized approach to civic education buttressed the valorization of economic productivity, social order, and stability over the protection of human rights and social justice. Government leaders in Asia further justified the de-politicization of academic spaces by propagating stereotypes and essentialisms about Asian societies as purportedly harmonious and averse to controversy and dissent. To address the limitations of neoliberal and nation-centric paradigms of reform on civic education, Alviar-Martin and Baildon recommended as central to an extensive and transformative GCE the inclusion of economic, political, and social justice issues, and commitments to ending poverty, protecting the earth, and supporting greater diversity and democratic deliberation in classrooms and society.

Ispandriarno and Löffelholz looked into how the growth of Indonesia's trade industry and its integration into the global economy have yet to provide impetus for the further expansion, quality enhancement, and internationalization of tertiary education. While top-tier institutions have actively engaged in internationalization, they noted that the majority of the universities in the country remained reluctant to adapt to the changing education landscape. As well, responses to the challenges of globalization among these universities differed immensely owing to student intake, teaching quality, service missions, disparate levels of readiness to conduct research, and responsiveness to the labor market. Focusing on the case of Universitas Atma Jaya Yogyakarta (UAJY), a top performing higher education institution, Ispandriarno and Löffelholz discussed in detail processes it undertook to internationalize. They concluded that commitment to pursue reforms with a view toward global competitiveness was not adequate; it necessitated strong leadership, mechanisms for reviewing, recognizing, and rewarding staff development for internationalization, and ample resources.

An analysis of the effects of globalization on education likewise called for an investigation of experiences from marginalized regions. Lorenzana and Rodriguez's chapter described how a university in Cotabato City in the Autonomous Region of Muslim Mindanao (ARMM) initiated a research collaboration program with a top university in Manila to enhance research output. The program centered on creating avenues for collaboration and consisted of an informal mentoring component that encouraged researchers from the university in Cotabato to increase their research output. While measures to sustain the program and maintain open channels of communication were put in place, class, gender, and age differences, and attitudes toward authority confounded collaboration and mentoring efforts. Asymmetrical power relations and status disparities, added Lorenzana and Rodriguez, also made it difficult to sustain collaborative relationships. Administrative duties and the lack of competency in scholarly writing were obstacles as well.

Guevarra also shed light on the role of the margins in globalizing education. She attributed as an outcome of the global turn the increasing tendency among writers from "smaller countries" to write for an international audience. Studying the works of Asian novelists Murakami Haruki, Kim Young-ha, and FH Batacan, she maintained that global literature, after all, had a transnational and transcultural character that necessitated the inclusion and consideration of literature from the peripheries. In arguing for their inclusion, Guevarra viewed Asian postcolonial experiences, episodes that usually highlighted domination and transgressions by some outside power, as important in expanding the breadth and scope of global literature.

Yet the inclusion of these texts also required the writers to be fluent or competent in English, a fact that Guevarra saw as instrumental in the creation of a niche for the practice of translation to become an industry. She added that publishing houses, international conglomerates, and influential proponents of economic and cultural globalization, have benefited immensely from this growing industry.

Universities, added Guevarra, have likewise been instrumental in enhancing global literature's reach through class syllabi that included peripheral writers' works. On the one hand, teaching global literature meant creating spaces for students to appreciate cultural diversity. On the other, however, the handling of these texts might lead to the erasure of cultural nuances that made them unique, a likelihood she cautioned against and suggested as a pitfall of both translation and pedagogy in the context of globalization.

Meanwhile, Nebres viewed as problematic the propensity of Asian universities to adhere to North American and Western European standards in implementing internationalization strategies intended to promote competitiveness. While these strategies are undeniably important, the Jesuit mathematician cautioned against neglecting other models of education reform, most notably approaches informed by diverse Asian experiences, when pursuing initiatives meant to engender stronger research capabilities and better university rankings. He argued for an approach that balances competitiveness and relevance while emphasizing the role of the latter in addressing some of the detrimental effects of educational development. Promoting relevance, contended Nebres, partly means recognizing that some Asian countries tread paths of development at a much slower pace than others. For instance, the Philippines could learn from Japan, which works on a 12-year curricular change cycle. This process, shared Nebres, requires the gathering and consolidation of feedback from actual classroom experiences at the district, provincial, and national level. It could likewise find lessons from the Vietnamese experience, which identifies committed leadership, a focused curriculum, and steady investment in teachers as important in ensuring exemplary student performance.

Arao noted the absence of a new paradigm in dealing with the effects of globalization on the Philippine education system. He expounded on Nebres' observations by arguing that prevailing approaches to produce globally competitive academic institutions, strategies governed by principles of deregulation, liberalization, and privatization, have not been successful in creating inclusive education institutions. Instead, these initiatives have reproduced existing inequalities. For instance, Department of Education (DepEd) data in 2013 showed that only seven out of ten pupils were capable of completing grade school in the country, and out of the seven, only five students could finish secondary education. Arao further revealed that access to education was even more problematic at the tertiary level since a little more than one-fifth of prospective students belonging to the 16-to-21-year-old cohort actually managed to enroll. He also argued how the Philippine government's strong adherence to global standards of academic excellence has spawned an elitist education system that further exudes a colonial and feudal character. He identified as indicators of the growing corporatization of education the use of English as a medium of instruction, the subordination of schools to profit-making ventures, and prohibitive school-related expenses notwithstanding the provision of free tuition in public elementary and high schools.

The studies of Alviar-Martin and Baildon, and Ispandriarno and Löffelholz illustrate in many ways institutional changes that have been prevalent across Asian educational institutions. These changes reflect what Nebres and Arao astutely noted as a strong endorsement of Western standards of academic excellence, an unfettered trend in the region. Afforded critical attention were administrative, curricular, and pedagogical reforms that were meant to position Asian education institutions better as global competitors. These papers further revealed how diverse and oftentimes conflicting understandings of internationalization and local school practices hampered the implementation of reforms. The challenges of acquiescing to dominant Western models of education reform were central to the arguments of Lorenzana and Rodriguez, and Nebres who focused on the effects of globalization on marginalized stakeholders of education. They argued against policy copying, which belied a haphazard approach and an uncritical appreciation of education reform.

Altogether, these papers contribute to the robust knowledge being produced on the impact of globalization on education systems in Asia. As Mok (2007) and, to a certain extent, Qiang (2003) demonstrated, the strong adherence of Asian education institutions to Western standards and strategies in promoting global competitiveness and academic excellence appears to be inevitable, a major cause being the lack of alternative paradigms informed by experiences of education reform in Asian localities. Substantial knowledge, in fact, has been generated on the immense implications of Western-style restructuring on school administration, curriculum and pedagogy, and research to name a few. But perhaps the plurality of perspectives on internationalization also warrants a more critical and nuanced appreciation of heretofore cursorily examined ways by which education stakeholders in Asia understand globalization, cope with the increasing demands to internationalize, and find creative means of managing its effects.

References

Collins, R. (2002). Credential inflation and the future of universities. In S.G. Brint (Ed.), *The future of the city of intellect: The changing American university* (pp. 23-46). Palo Alto, CA: Stanford University Press.

Mok, K. H. (2007). Questing for internationalization of universities in Asia: Critical reflections. *Journal of Studies in International Education, 11*(3/4), 433-454.

Qiang, Z. (2003). Internationalization of higher education: Towards a conceptual framework. *Policy Futures in Education, 1*(2), 248-270.

*

Theresa B. Alviar-Martin
Mark C. Baildon

Issues-Centered Global Citizenship Education in Asia

Theoretical Discourses and Curricular Considerations*

SINCE 2001 the British Broadcasting Corporation (BBC) has commissioned an annual survey on global citizenship as part of its World Service's *Identity* series (GlobeScan 2016). Among the survey items, one asks participants to respond to the statement "I see myself more as a global citizen than a citizen of my country." The 2016 study involved over 20,000 participants from 21 countries, and for the first time since the survey's implementation, over half of the respondents (51%) indicated that they identified "strongly" or "somewhat" as global citizens. Notably, three of four surveyed Asian nations returned responses above the international mean in identifying primarily as global citizens as opposed to citizens of their nation, including China (71%), India (67%), and Pakistan (56%).

The BBC's findings echo a growing interest in global citizenship since the start of the 21st century. Despite its ubiquity, "global

---

* The paper, presented at the Eighth Ateneo International Conference on Asian Studies, draws from a review published in 2016 in Curriculum Perspectives (36) 2. The review is part of a series of studies supported by the Hong Kong University Grants Council (GRF Project 18602115).

citizenship" and ideas on how to educate students for global citizenship remain hotly contested topics. The historical role of civic education as preparing young people to know the rights, responsibilities, and duties accorded to citizens of their nations (Hahn and Alviar-Martin 2008; Heater 2003), renders education for global citizenship an especially contentious field (Myers 2016). However, scholars and educators agree that young citizens need to be equipped to address the problems confronting a globalized and interconnected world (Osler and Starkey 2005; UNESCO 2014). Among the issues that challenge the human community are environmental degradation, global pandemics, income inequality, and more recently, the rise of exclusionary rhetoric amidst increasing cultural diversity in societies. As part of the United Nations Educational, Scientific, and Cultural Organization (UNESCO) *Decade of Education for Sustainable Development*, UNESCO released the 2014 Report on Global Citizenship Education (GCE), defining GCE as an educational framing paradigm that aims to develop the knowledge, skills, values, and attitudes learners need for securing a world which is more just, peaceful, tolerant, inclusive, secure, and sustainable. The report installs global issues as an organizing impetus. "Encouraging learners to analyze real-life issues critically and to identify possible solutions creatively and innovatively" appears as the first aim of GCE, and three subsequent objectives state that students will be able to identify the assumptions, actions, and collaboration skills that are "necessary supports to the study of global issues" (UNESCO 2014: 9).

The growing visibility of GCE and urgency of addressing global issues resonate with the conference's theme of examining "Education for a Globalizing Asia," which compels us to ponder transnational flows of ideas, the global exchange of pedagogical practices, and the shaping of education policies in the region. This paper focuses on GCE policies in Asia and specifically, these policies' implications on issues-centered curriculum development and practice. Research in Asian societies attests to recognition of the importance of issues-centered pedagogy (Cogan 1997; Kennedy, Lee, and Grossman 2010; Lee 2009). Yet, scholars contend that ideological discourses and educational policies that subsume global citizenship within neoliberal and nation-centric frameworks of reform hamper efforts towards issues-centered GCE

(Gaudelli 2009; Myers 2016). In this paper, we review empirical studies from Asia to illustrate how issues-centered GCE unfolds and is influenced by these dominant discourses, in many ways resulting in a type of civic education that disenfranchises and alienates young citizens.

This paper is organized into three sections. Initially, we situate GCE amidst theoretical discourses of global citizenship. Second, we draw on theories of global discourses as we share findings from a review of civic education policies in three Asian societies. Finally, we outline several implications for curriculumplanning and practice. By examining the ways that discourses of GCE are apparent in Asian societies' educational reform policies, this paper aims to illuminate global influences and resulting contextual tensions, so as to contribute to efforts towards issues-centered and transformative GCE.

Discourses of GCE and the issues-centered global curriculum

Discourses are ways of constituting knowledge, the language and beliefs that serve as frameworks and ideologies to help orient people's understanding and actions in the world (Foucault 1980). Abowitz and Harnish (2006: 655) illustrated the ways that curriculum is a discursive practice reflective of "terminology, values, rhetorical styles, habits, and truths" that spring from historical and social conditions. They argued that stated intentions in the civic curriculum—found in official documents articulating appropriate modes of civic engagement or political directives that define civic identity—comprise expressions of beliefs about citizenship, privileging specific ideological perspectives over others. In light of transnational exchanges of ideas that are informing curriculum policies across societies (Steiner-Khamsi 2010), Gaudelli (2009) identified cosmopolitanism, nationalism, and neoliberalism as global ideological discourses surrounding GCE. Each ideology differentially shapes civic curriculum outcomes and implicates the manner in which teachers and learners approach the study of global issues.

GCE as defined by UNESCO (2014) echoes the cosmopolitan perspective in that it recognizes "the moral obligations owed to all human beings based solely on (their) humanity alone, without reference to race, gender, nationality, ethnicity, culture, religion, political affiliation, state citizenship, or other communal particularities" (Brown and Held 2010: 1). *Cosmopolitanism* acknowledges individuals' capacities to form overlapping affiliations, attachments, and consciousness (Banks 2008) that are foundations of an ability to approach ideas from multiple perspectives (Hanvey 1976). Given the richness and multiplicity of individuals' identities, cosmopolitan GCE considers learners as contributors of knowledge. The Octagon model of the International Association of Educational Achievement's Civic Education Study mirrors theories of learning within the cosmopolitan perspective, capturing the ways in which school, community, national, and transnational discourses influence the civic curriculum while emphasizing students' agency to construct personal meanings of citizenship within these intersecting communities of discourse and practice (Torney-Purta et al. 2001).

Appiah (2008: 95) further positions the idea of "fallibility" as a foundation of the cosmopolitan perspective. Fallibility posits that individuals are charged with ultimate responsibility for their own lives, but insists that each person reflects on whether or not they are doing their fair share to "make sure everyone has the chance at the dignified human existence that we are all entitled to." Ultimately, the goal of cosmopolitan GCE is the transformation of the individual as well as society based on principles of equality, social justice, and human rights (Hicks 2003; Osler and Starkey 2005; UNESCO 2014). Thus, the consideration of societal problems through systemic and political frameworks is central to the GCE curriculum (UNESCO 2014). This entails cultivating in students the skills of reflection, criticality, collaboration, and problem-solving as they examine the ways that "political issues and actors shape the local, familiar world around them" (Myers 2016: 4).

Cosmopolitanism remains at the periphery of the GCE ideological landscape (Oxley and Morris 2013). Rather, GCE is dominated by discourses of nationalism and neoliberalism (Gaudelli 2009; Myers 2016). Traditionally, theorists posit curriculum as a form of "institutionalized learning" whose structure, sequence, and outcomes are strongly associated with discourses of development particular to nation-states (Reid 2003). The national perspective of GCE builds on Western liberal and republican political traditions in positing civic identity as primarily a matter of social contract between the state and the individual (Abowitz and Harnish, 2006). It aims towards a shared national identity among diverse populations, and employs logics of national security and anti-terrorism (Parker 2011) as means to strengthen the nation's standing in a highly competitive, unequal, and politically volatile world. Because nationalist discourses reflect hierarchies entrenched in states' political and social systems, powerful sectors of society decide the knowledge, skills, and capacities that are worth learning (Apple 1990). The nation's dominant identities and economic priorities, therefore, frame students' learning about the world (Spring 2004), and the study of global issues follows a path towards "predetermined, conventionally-conceived cultural and social spaces" (Zong, Wilson, and Quashiga 2008: 203).

The neoliberal ideology, on the other hand, contends that national governments and institutions have "reinvented themselves as global entities in order to survive in a global economy" (Gaudelli 2009: 71). People are reconfigured to become conversant in the homogenization and hybridity brought by globalization, and their participation in capital, either as investor, consumer, or entrepreneur, constitutes an act of citizenship. Applied to education, neoliberalism is evident in standards-based reforms, high-stake examinations and ranking, international comparisons, and discourses focused on excellence (Davies and Bansel 2007; Gaudelli, 2009). Thus, similar to the nationalist perspective, neoliberalism limits classroom-based exploration of societal issues because it implies knowledge that is scientifically-based, transferrable, measurable, and objective (Eisner 2002; Gaudelli 2010).

The skills of innovation, criticality, or problem-solving that are fundamental to an issues-centered pedagogy may be evident in the neoliberal curriculum; however, these are couched within rationalizations such as preparation for work or addressing demands in the global economy.

The context of GCE in Asia: policy, curriculum, and pedagogy

Cosmopolitan principles are evident in cultural and religious traditions of Asian societies (Sen 2010). As scholars have noted, across Islam, Confucianism, and Buddhism are provisions to educate young people to care for the fate of human beings inside and outside their own societies, to value cultural diversity, and to develop skills for dialogue across differences (Appiah 2006; Nussbaum 2012). Research likewise notes the presence of cosmopolitan principles in educational reform intentions across Asia. For example, Lee (2009: 18), in a survey of studies conducted by the Comparative Education Research Center (CERC), described official intentions for citizenship education in the region as tending to "emphasise democratic values, and advocate that citizenship teaching should be...characterised by dialogue and critical thinking." However, affirming theories of global curriculum discourses, GCE in Asia is subsumed within education policies geared towards national and economic development that overshadow cosmopolitan perspectives (UNESCO 2014).

A report on Transversal Education (UNESCO 2013) focused on global citizenship and three other key dimensions (critical and innovative thinking, inter-personal skills, and intra-personal skills) is a case in point. The study involved nine Asian jurisdictions (China [Shanghai], Hong Kong, India, Japan, Republic of Korea, Malaysia, Mongolia, the Philippines, and Thailand). The researchers reported the predominance of critical and innovative thinking relative to the other key dimensions. They also noted the influence of "social and humanistic discourses" in fostering national identity while cultivating attributes reflective of cosmopolitan principles, such as respect for diversity, tolerance, and empathy. Yet, "economic discourses" embodied in rationales such as "boosting economic development and increasing international competitiveness" and addressing "the changing demands of the workplace" proved to be "the most powerful driver" of education reform (UNESCO 2013: 6).

Global citizenship education curriculum in Asia is likewise shaped by emphasis on moral virtues and personal values (Kennedy and Fairbrother 2004) that reinforce the convergence of moral and civic education. Unlike civic education in the West that pertains to knowledge, skills, and attitudes necessary for individuals to function as members of the polity, moral education is concerned primarily with the cultivation of virtues towards ethical behavior (Kennedy and Fairbrother 2004). Many Asian citizenship curricula, however, merge moral and civic education into one subject, based on the premise that cultivating ethics and values is fundamental in the preparation of good citizens (Lee 2006). Thus, learning about the world is framed by depoliticized constructions of citizenship. For example, research involving 12 Asian jurisdictions (Bhutan, Brunei, China [Shanghai], Hong Kong, Indonesia, Japan, Republic of Korea, Malaysia, the Philippines, Singapore, Thailand, Mongolia) found that formal education initiatives in the region interpreted GCE as a moral rather than political endeavor (UNESCO 2014).

Aside from the predominantly depoliticized approach to civic education, the tenacity of nationalist discourses shapes the regional contours of GCE in Asia. Ong (1999) argues that depoliticized forms of moral/civic education reinforce neoliberal and nationalist policies that place economic productivity and the order and stability desired by the nation-state above the protection of human rights or social justice. She further contends that government leaders in Asia have employed stereotypical "Orientalist essentialisms" (1999: 81) and a "Confucian cultural triumphalism" (Ong 2006: 135) as sources of instrumental rationality. The "Asian values" of meritocracy, hard work, respect for authority, and social harmony have been used to create a disciplined labor force that appeals to global capital in the service of the nation-state (Ong 2006).

Lee's (2009) survey of citizenship education in Asia points to how the nationalistic ideology's spheres of influence extend beyond policies and curricular intentions to the ways that teachers enact the curriculum. Stressing that teachers do not blindly follow the intended curriculum, but instead choose pedagogies that "best fit a combination of contextual factors and learning situations," Lee (2009) identified three orientations that combine to create "hybridized" forms of civic education pedagogies. *Globally-oriented* and *personally-oriented pedagogies* reflect cosmopolitan principles, in that the former promotes democracy and critical thinking, and is progressive, dialogic, and rationalistic; whereas the latter "attends to the development of citizenship values and attributes from within the person" through experiential learning, reflection, and connections to daily life (Lee 2009: 20). In contrast, *nation-oriented pedagogies* are "didactic, inculcating, persuasive, expository, content-based, exam-oriented, and conservative" (2009: 21). Although these orientations intersect in teachers' pedagogies, nation-centric orientations tend to prevail, creating a repertoire of practices that Lee (2009) describes as politically neutral or depoliticized, encouraging community service, stressing respect for family and government leaders, and oriented towards building national identity.

Scenarios of issues-centered GCE in Asian societies

Given the complex interplay of global discourses at the policy, curriculum, and pedagogical levels, we sought to gain a situated understanding of issues-centered GCE by reviewing empirical studies from selected Asian societies. In the following section, we discuss the cases of Singapore, Bhutan, and Japan to highlight the collision of discourses and implications to issues-centered GCE. Our aim was not to generalize the nature of GCE in the region. Rather, by examining the three cases, we sought to illuminate different national responses to perceived problems wrought by globalization. Our review of studies was guided by the following questions: a) What issues does the official curriculum identify as important? b) What discourses are employed to rationalize these issues? c) How are these issues taught? Figure 1 illustrates the discursive influences on the intended curriculum in the three societies. Similar to Lee's (2009) observations, Figure 1 depicts the prevalence of nation-centric and morally-grounded discourses in policy and curricular intentions; however, in each society we noted differing responses to neoliberal and cosmopolitan discourses.

Figure 1

Discursive scenarios of GCE

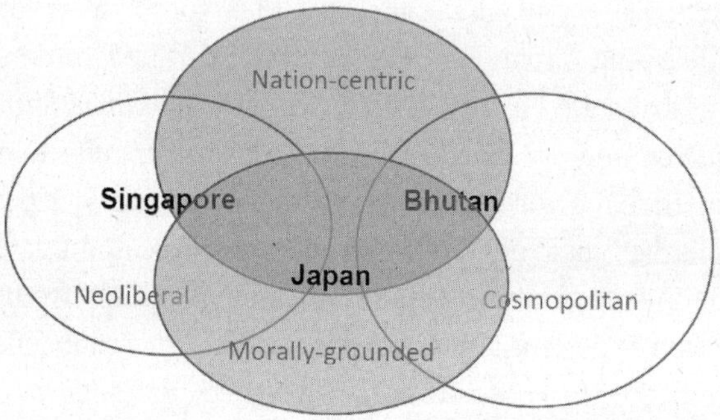

Singapore: Instrumental GCE

The case of Singapore captures an instrumental type of GCE that builds on depoliticized and nationalistic forms of civic identity while drawing on neoliberal discourses in constructing citizens as adaptable workers. The 2000 Report of the Committee on Compulsory Education (CCE) (MOE 2000: 2) encapsulates the intersection of these three discourses, noting that the curriculum aims to develop a common core of knowledge and skills to "build national identity and social cohesion" and "prepare students for the global economy." Towards these ends, civic education forwards a narrative of national vulnerability and the need to inoculate the nation from perceived threats brought by globalization (Gopinathan 2007).

Policies and curricular documents convey a sense of vulnerability as central to national history by citing social unrest brought about by struggles against communists and labor unions in the early years of national independence. More recently, official discourse has emphasized Singapore's exposure to external shocks, such as the Asian financial crisis of 1997, pandemic diseases, intense global competition, and foreign values and lifestyles (Daipi 2002). Thus, although civic education subjects (i.e. Social Studies and National Education) feature the study of global issues, many highlight the need to "learn from other countries' experiences to build and sustain a politically viable, socially cohesive and economically vibrant Singapore" (MOE 2008) while reiterating how globalization and the changing global economy might "strain the loyalties and attachments of young Singaporeans" (Gopinathan, 2007: 61). For example, the 2008 GCE Ordinary Level Social Studies syllabus for secondary students is organized around two core ideas: *Being Rooted* and *Living Globally*. Three themes develop the idea of living globally. *Managing International Relations* and *Sustaining Economic Development* use Singapore as an example to describe "the defence and security of nations and how friendships are cultivated among nations ... to build a politically stable and economically vibrant community" (2007: 8). The final theme, *Facing Challenges and Change,* examines the rise and fall of medieval Venice to illustrate how nations overcome challenges in order to survive.

Singapore's instrumental approach limits the enactment of issues-centered GCE in several ways. For one, skills that are foundational to the study of global issues, such as critical thinking or problem-solving, are constructed primarily as marketable skills necessary to compete in the workforce (Alviar-Martin and Baildon 2016). Second, the government provides "out-of-bound markers" to signal sensitive topics that might undermine social cohesion, and studies show that teachers have practiced self-censorship or avoided sensitive issues such as sexuality, abortion, or political controversies (Ho, Alviar-Martin, and Leviste 2014). Research further illustrates how students differentially experience GCE based on academic tracking within a stratified system of schooling (Ho, Alviar-Martin, Sim, and Yap 2011). Founded on a paternalistic political culture where government leadership is drawn from an elite intelligentsia (Baildon, Sim, and Paculdar 2014), Singapore employs systems of meritocracy to identify high-achieving learners capable of leading the nation through global challenges. Academic tracking extends to types of global knowledge and competencies where high achievers are prepared through a globally-focused civic education that develops higher-order thinking and leadership skills, whereas the lowest achievers experience a locally-focused, technical skills-based curriculum (Ho 2012). Such a system provides a pre-sorted workforce with increasing disparities between upper and lower income-earners, and a diminishing middle class (Sassen 2014).

The focus on instrumentalist skills development that characterizes neoliberal and nation-centric GCE prepares young people to work productively in stratified national and global economies, but fails to acknowledge fully other forms of identity, agency, affiliation, or aspirations available to young people in Singapore. It will not prepare students – especially students in lower academic tracks – to think critically about complex issues central to living in a diverse global society, such as issues pertaining to human rights, climate change, or social justice since they do not have opportunities to deliberate these in the official curriculum. Students may have difficulty seeing themselves aligned with the interests of those who are different than themselves in terms of nationality or even with their fellow citizens sorted along socio-economic lines in the workforce.

Young citizens may not fully develop the capacities necessary to recognize their shared humanity with those who are different than themselves or address issues that cross national boundaries (or even those of social class, race, or gender) in ways that are just and ethical.

Bhutan: Spiritual GCE

The second scenario of GCE combines morally-grounded, nation-centric, and cosmopolitan discourses to emphasize the need for spiritual development, and is captured by the policy of Gross National Happiness (GNH) and Values Education (VE) in Bhutan. Spiritual global citizenship constructs the world as an interdependent system, where individual and societal well-being are dependent upon responsible economic development that considers spiritual enrichment and harmonious co-existence with nature (Lokamitra 2004). As opposed to the instrumental orientation, Bhutan's spirituality-based GCE critiques traditional measures of gross domestic production as flawed in that these "promote limitless growth in a world that is finite" (UN News Center 2012), and points to the excesses of economic competition as sources of self-centeredness, materialism, and social disharmony (Wangyal 2001).

Bhutan's GNH policy reflects the nation's Mahayana Buddhist heritage and agricultural-based economy. It seeks a "holistic, inclusive, equitable and sustainable" type of progress, where "political and spiritual matters (are) in balance" (Tschering 2010). The *Vision 2020* policy expresses values central to education as a critical driver of GNH. The policy aims to "ensure the realization of the innate potential of every child; instill an awareness of the nation's unique cultural heritage, and values, both traditional and universal; prepare young people for the world of work, instilling in them the dignity of labour; and create an awareness of the potential and importance of agriculture as an occupation" (Zam 2008: 5). Thus, the pursuit of GNH through values education fosters the Bhutanese national identity (Royal Government of Bhutan 2011). The emphasis on GNH requires citizens to consider economic development as a "moral space that includes all human interaction, and to treat the other members of society not as opponents in a bargaining contest but as co-citizens of a shared *res publica* and as moral subjects which are to be respected in exercising one's own freedom" (Hirata, 2004: 724).

Bhutan's civic education framework advocates a shared civic morality in terms of compassion, non-violence, and harmony with nature and others (Wangyal 2001). Along with the VE curriculum, the framework conveys arguably cosmopolitan principles in that these delineate the conduct of interpersonal relationships and the responsibility of all sentient beings (Lokamitra 2004). The VE curriculum centers around fundamental Tibetan/Bhutanese concepts that underline how good begets good, the importance of doing good, and the impermanence of life (*ley judrey*), as well as building of mutual trust in a relationship-oriented society (*tha damtshing*) (Sakurai 2011). These and other values of respect for family and friends, karma, and non-violence appear in the early primary years and are revisited in Grades 4-6, through topics such as "bullying," "how to protect the planet," "international charities," "local democracy," and "stories in newspapers: facts, opinions, and different versions" (Sakurai, 2011, p. 181).

Beyond the coverage of content, the VE curriculum shows little evidence of how topics might be discussed as issues and deliberated after consideration of multiple perspectives, which are important facets of cosmopolitanism. Rather, the curriculum is unambiguously teacher-centered, with teachers traditionally expected to impart knowledge and "help the student overcome his ignorance" (Wangyal 2001: 5). The state's transmissive model of values education and emerging efforts to evaluate the effectiveness of GNH forward a type of learning that is lacking in critical thinking. For example, in order for their school to be recognized as an official GNH school, teachers must abide by 17 "attitudinal cautions" such as being "morally, culturally, and politically correct in language/ speech," and "not talk(ing) ill about others" (Sakurai 2011: 182). The organizing paradigm of happiness—coupled with narrow delineations of teaching and learning—call into question the transformative potential of GCE in Bhutan. As Sakurai (2011: 183) observed, Bhutan seems to be "legitimating GNH-infused education in order to fortify national identity as a more cohesive nation-state...whereby the government tries to strengthen its power over the people".

Japan: Humanistic GCE

The third scenario, humanistic GCE, is positioned at the intersection of morally-grounded, nation-centric, neoliberal, and cosmopolitan discourses. Humanistic GCE acknowledges the need for national participation in the global economy; however, its constructions of "the global" recognize threats posed by globalization on human relations. Citing the deterioration of social relationships, the loss of identity, and rising global terrorism, humanistic GCE calls for the cultivation of values, increased recognition of social and cultural rights, and a renewed civic purpose within societies. It is exemplified by recent civic education reform efforts in Japan.

Historically, Japan has straddled two opposing conceptions of citizenship. The term, *"kohmin"* represents the official definition of citizenship, and is used by government textbooks in referring to an authorized or legal status of a member of the state. On the other hand, *"shimin"* is commonly used in media and society. It connotes a membership in civil society and emphasizes participation in NGOs, human rights issues, or matters of social justice (Otsu 2009). Citizenship education has consisted traditionally of two courses (Social Studies and Moral Education) that, for many years, faced criticism as being disjointed and predominated by *kohmin* as a framing paradigm. However, a series of policy initiatives brought attention to problems confronting Japanese society that paved the way for civic education reform, and arguably, reconciled the two notions of citizenship.

The *Report of the Central Council for Education* (MEXT 2003), *The Basic Plan for the Promotion of Education* (MEXT 2008), and *The Second Basic Plan for the Promotion of Education* (MEXT 2013a) laid the basis of education reform. Collectively, these documents cite over 20 years of economic stagnation, an ageing population, *anomie* and youth alienation, and "weakened educational functions of families and local communities and the tendency for people to feel difficulty in finding a sense of purpose or motivation" (MEXT 2013a). Based on these challenges, MEXT called for holistic reform towards an "education-based society" necessary to develop social competencies for survival and "individuals who create change and new values." Accompanying this overarching vision was the Revisions of the Courses of Study (MEXT 2006) with the primary aim of developing character and civic-mindedness by emphasizing "soft power"—such as rediscovering Japanese traditions and culture and by highlighting "a zest for life"—so that citizens could actively participate in state and community affairs and help develop a more democratic and peaceful society (MEXT 2013b).

Under these reforms, two of the three civic education subjects (Social Studies, Moral Education, and the newly-introduced Integrated Studies) were adjusted to include more opportunities for students to investigate issues confronting society. Recognizing the importance of students' connections to their local communities, MEXT allowed schools to create their own Integrated Studies curricula. Among guidelines given to teachers were to design interdisciplinary themes that a) children were interested in; b) corresponded to particular characteristics of the school community; and c) spanned the environment, international relations, welfare, and technology. Teachers were encouraged to attempt problem-solving activities, experiments, visits to the local community, and collaborative endeavors that engaged children of different ages (Otsu 2009).

The Social Studies curriculum similarly includes the study of societal problems and controversial issues (Yoshimura 2011), and states that students will be "interested in society..., consider events from various perspectives based on data..., (and) deepen understanding and love for their nation and history" (Otsu 2009). In contrast to these two subjects, Moral Education has retained a more didactic pedagogical approach towards several aims, such as helping students a) cultivate respect for human beings, b) nurture a richness of the heart, and c) succeed in developing traditional culture and a rich culture. Although taught for only one hour a week, it functions as a subject that consolidates and outweighs learnings from other subjects (Sakurai 2011).

Scholars have voiced concern regarding reforms to the three civic education subjects. On one hand, Integrated Studies and Social Studies have faced criticism for difficulties encountered by teachers in creating meaningful activities that encourage critical thinking, the acquisition of complex social knowledge, and well-considered social judgment in solving problems in society (Yoshimura 2011), whereas Moral Education has been decried for its patriotic construction of values, keeping students from thinking critically about what defines the nation and its tendency to substitute "psychological issues for critical issues in society" (Otsu 2009: 83).

Discussion: enacting cosmopolitan ideals as practices of transformative GCE curricula

The cases of Singapore, Bhutan, and Japan demonstrate three different educational responses taken by nations in the face of globalization. These are, respectively, the adoption of instrumentalist, spiritual, and humanistic approaches to GCE. The extent to which official discourses and curriculum policies in all three nations support GCE, however, merits closer scrutiny.

Singapore

The focus on instrumentalist skills development that characterizes Singapore's neoliberal and nation-centric GCE aims to prepare young people to work productively in stratified national and global economies. Although the nation-state in Singapore has recently taken on more redistributionist social policies to shield citizens from the vagaries of globalization and to maintain political stability, the narrow view of students and citizens as human capital fails to acknowledge other forms of identity, agency, affiliation, and aspirations that Singaporeans may have. Singapore's students—especially those in lower academic tracks—have few opportunities in the official curriculum to deliberate about complex issues central to living in a diverse global society, such as human rights and social justice issues. Situated in the context of preparing students for achievement on high-stakes exams and global economic competitiveness, an instrumental GCE designed to develop productive citizens wedded to the nation-state doesn't acknowledge the political dimensions of GCE (Myers 2016).

Bhutan

In the case of Bhutan, the nation-state has rejected the neoliberal goals fervently pursued by Singapore. Instead, the emphasis on Gross National Happiness, spirituality, and values education seems to mark a very different vision of GCE. However, upon closer analysis, GCE discourse and practice in Bhutan remain nation-centric and depoliticized. It is a national response to globalization that is morally grounded and attempts to promote values education as a form of national ballast against globalizing forces that threaten Bhutanese culture. Although it offers a more balanced and holistic approach to citizenship development grounded in Bhutan's cultural heritage and traditional values, the dignity of labor, sustainable progress, spirituality, and respect for nature, it too falls short of preparing students for the political dimensions of GCE by framing values and GNH as non-negotiable. In limiting the ways that schools are able to enact GNH, and by emphasizing transmissive teaching rather than pedagogies that encourage the viewing of GNH policies and traditional values through multiple perspectives, the case of Bhutan reveals a different type of depoliticized GCE that may fail to adequately prepare students to understand and address the complex economic and political dimensions of global issues.

Japan

Sakurai (2011: 183) compares Bhutan's GNH-infused education with the educational reforms initiated by Japan's 2006 Fundamental Law by noting that they were both initiatives of new political regimes to "fortify national identity as a more cohesive nation-state." Like Singapore and Bhutan, education policy in Japan is designed to manage threats posed by globalization, especially in the realm of social relationships and well-being. While officials in Japan are deeply concerned about *anomie* and youth alienation, they are also concerned about lingering economic stagnation and the need to revitalize Japanese identity and society by a return to traditional culture and values. The two distinct definitions of citizenship that operate in Japan—one articulating legal membership and identity to the state and the other emphasizing social relations—provide the impetus for new citizenship education efforts that focus more on humanistic goals. These include more student-centered pedagogical approaches, the study of societal problems and controversial issues, and greater respect for traditional culture and diversity. Similar to Bhutan, the inward embrace of traditional culture and values constitutes efforts to strengthen national identity and unity in uncertain global contexts (Sakurai 2011) but does little to empower young people to work across national contexts to take action on the shared problems that face humanity.

If we return to Appiah's (2008) notion of fallibility as central to cosmopolitanism and GCE, we begin with the premise that our knowledge (individually and collectively) is necessarily limited, that we are likely to be mistaken about a great many things. This is true for citizens, including government officials, policy makers, and curriculum designers. This means as citizens and educators, we benefit from contact with diverse others who can help us become more aware of the limitations in our own views and knowledge. As Appiah (2008: 86) puts it, "we can borrow good ideas from all over the world, not just from within our own society. It's worth listening to others because they may have something to teach us; it's worth their listening to us, because they may have something to learn." We have a great deal to learn from diverse others. Engaging with others, being respectful of difference, and being willing to participate in dialogue and conversation to learn with and from others are key principles. These guiding principles, fundamental to both education and citizenship, can guide a re-envisioning of GCE within different national contexts.

The lens of fallibility helps us see that nation-centric discourses and approaches, although well-intentioned by national officials concerned about the fate of their nation-state and their citizens in challenging global contexts, will always be limited in their vision and scope of GCE. A growing body of research points to the dominance (and limits) of nationalist and neoliberal discourses with critical and cosmopolitan discourses at the periphery in the ways GCE is conceptualized and enacted (e.g., Abowitz and Harnish 2006; Alviar-Martin and Baildon 2016; Davies and Bansel 2007; Gaudelli 2009). Increasing social polarization, the marginalization of alternative perspectives, and a sense of political disenfranchisement among certain segments of society, including youth, means that a range of views and forms of knowledge and participation are being left out of the equation of education policy and curriculum formulation.

How, then, can cosmopolitan and attendant critical perspectives be made more visible in curriculum practice? The curriculum theorist, Joseph Schwab (1969), forwarded one such approach in his model of "the practical." Although writing about curriculum inquiry and development writ large, Schwab discussed principles by which practitioners might view GCE reform efforts beyond narratives of formal education as producing a set of transferrable behaviors, knowledge, and attitudes, towards a practice that illuminates how global issues implicate local and quotidian social and political realities. Schwab (1969: 502) suggested ways by which "agents of translation" can consider the global through deliberation over several commonplaces: the milieu, subject matter, learners, and teachers.

The *milieu* calls attention to the school and classroom in which learning occurs: the contexts and structures of authority within these settings, the relationships between students, adults and students, and teachers and educational leaders. Beyond the school setting, the milieu includes the students' families and community, as well as broader ideological, political, social, and economic contexts. Within these contexts, what global forces are in play? How do global forces shape the school's and community's struggles and aspirations, daily economic realities, dominant preoccupations, and cultural climate? Notably, curriculum developers for GCE would take these questions into account in order to determine the role of policies in mediating the influence of global trends on the local milieu. It would help teachers make connections between school policies, their curriculum and students, and broader contexts—and the way the global is implicated in each.

The second commonplace refers to the nature of *subject matter*. Just as the identification and resolution of global problems served as the impetus for 21st century education reform, a globally-focused curriculum must install these issues as a central concern and basis of organization. Issues of political, social, and economic justice and commitments to ending poverty, protecting the earth, and supporting greater diversity and democratic deliberation in classrooms and society must be core subject matter if GCE is to fulfill its aspiration as a *transformative* tool (Noddings 2005; UNESCO 2014). The focus on issues within GCE curricula entails a move away from topics or discrete bodies of information. As revealed in the review of literature, recent standards-based reforms assume that academic knowledge is objective, neutral, and measurable (Gaudelli 2009). Heilman (2009) has critiqued entrenched positivist and modernist conceptions of knowledge that rest on "binary rational choices to determine the structures of the world" (Heilman 2009: 44). Citizenship curriculum is often fragmented along these binary choices, with knowledge seen as demarcated by traditional fields or disciplinary domains. Yet, cosmopolitan GCE requires curricula that install issues spanning multiple disciplines at the heart of learning and inquiry. Such a multidisciplinary and integrated curriculum not only calls into question the nature of knowledge, but also how learning is assessed. The compulsion to measure knowledge within a neoliberal platform of education reform and international competition

(Gaudelli 2009) contributes to the honoring of a slender range of cognitive processes, often relating to language, sequence, speech, and patterns (Eisner 2002). Meanwhile, those cognitive processes that are necessary ingredients in confronting complex societal issues and imagining novel solutions, "invention, boundary pushing, and boundary breaking" are usually neglected (Eisner 2002: 100).

Teachers comprise Schwab's third commonplace. Cosmopolitan forms of GCE operate from very different assumptions in which teaching is considered a political and moral activity that addresses issues of social justice and equity, with democratic deliberation a core practice. Thus, a re-envisioning of GCE compels teacher education to revisit the role of teachers as "curricular instructional gatekeepers" (Thornton 2005) who navigate a complex terrain of societal discourses and expectations, educational policy, and personal beliefs. Scholars argue that teachers must first learn to ponder their own attachments and identities before they can recognize how issues such as power and social-economic inequality influence their students' learning experiences and social and cultural realities (Merryfield 2000; Howard 2010). Further, international studies reveal that beyond building self-awareness, there is a need for teachers to examine how political, cultural, and economic principles have shaped what GCE is and what it should be (Zong, et al. 2008). This entails not only interrogating and analyzing the different ideologies that underpin education reforms, but also appreciating how their roles as teachers mediate neoliberal, nationalist, cosmopolitan, and other agendas.

Curriculum development for transformative and cosmopolitan GCE must also enable students to consider *learners* who are growing up in increasingly global and technology-mediated environments. All students are young citizens who bring with them certain biases, knowledge, aspirations, and identities that increasingly encompass both local and global affiliations. Key questions that cosmopolitan curricula ask are: "How do students define their identities?" and "What is the nature of their worldviews?" Learners' cultural, social, economic, and political backgrounds shape their ways of thinking and knowing the world, as well as their visions of an ideal society. A re-envisioned model of GCE, therefore, must equip teachers to determine the issues that matter to learners and how these issues play out in their everyday lives.

Beyond focus on curriculum development, policy makers and curriculum designers can invite stakeholders with different views and orientations to engage in policy and curriculum deliberation. Educators can create more spaces in curricula and classrooms for students to share and construct their own meanings about their roles as citizens in a globalized world (Alviar-Martin and Baildon 2016).

Policy deliberation, curriculum design, and classroom practice, then, can operate from these cosmopolitan principles to "raise basic questions about identity (who we are as citizens), membership (who belongs and the location of the boundaries), and agency (how we might best enact citizenship)" (Abowitz and Harnish 2006: 657). The cases presented in this article suggest that educators in different contexts also have much to learn from each other in envisioning different models of GCE.

Myers (2016) argues for GCE as a transformative practice that can provide opportunities for policy-makers, educators, and students to articulate and understand new types of relationships between the nation and its citizens as well as change our consciousness about the ways the world is experienced and interpreted. We argue that an issues-based GCE can be conceptualized as transformative practice by focusing on cosmopolitan ideals. Appiah (2008: 92) refers to cosmopolitanism as a "double-stranded tradition" of "universality plus difference". He argues that it's best "when people live by ideals they themselves believe in," instead of those ideals being imposed by others, but that we must remain open to different views and ways of doing things. We have to accept the idea that "our knowledge is imperfect, provisional, subject to revision in the face of new evidence" (2008: 96). It also entails recognizing that "everybody matters" and that we have "obligations to every other" (2008: 96). This makes matters of social justice central to GCE (e.g., the treatment of people, care for a shared environment, equity and equality, human rights and responsibilities, matters of governance, etc.).

Students must be given opportunities to investigate the moral, economic, psychological, and political dimensions of societal problems in order to develop key civic competencies (critical thought, public deliberation, perspective-taking, reflection, social action, etc.). Addressing these issues can be done at the local level, where the issues are most directly experienced in some form or another by local communities and students, but their study must directly confront issues of racism, classism, sexism, materialism, and militarism that are likely at their core. This requires that we "care about the fate of all our fellow human beings, not just the ones in our own political community" (2008: 86). This is a political and epistemological stance that involves an ethics of care, concern, and connection (Martin 1994) and certain moral competencies (Noddings 2005).

Clearly, these are not just principles for classroom practice, but entail a broader, more inclusive approach that will integrate political, civic, aesthetic, environmental, relational, ethical, and spiritual aspects of human experience. It is an approach that is aware of and works with different discourses, knowledge, and forms of social practice. As Gaudelli and Heilman (2009: 2672) note, "Understanding ourselves and our society, particularly in an increasingly global era in which localities are linked and fragmented through complex global ties, requires interdisciplinarity, spirituality, and criticality so that key Western, modernist, and market ways of understanding can be refined and improved."

GCE as transformative practice also requires the exercise of imagination, an openness to things *otherwise*. As the late activist Grace Lee Boggs (1998: 254) argues, "All over the world today we are obviously living in that in-between period of historical time when great numbers of people are aware that they cannot continue in the same old way but are immobilized because they cannot imagine an alternative". She highlights that imagining alternatives and bringing about real change will require people to "not only struggle against existing institutions. They must make a philosophical/spiritual leap and become more *human* human beings" (1998: 153). We believe the principles of cosmopolitan GCE that we outline, grounded in local, community-based issues and forms of civic agency, yet linked to broader issues and in solidarity with others who are different than ourselves, is a necessary step in this direction.

References

Abowitz, K. K., & Harnish, J. (2006). Contemporary discourses of citizenship. *Review of Educational Research, 76*(4), 653-690.

Alviar-Martin, T., & Baildon, M. C. (2016). Context and curriculum in two global cities: A study of discourses of citizenship in Hong Kong and Singapore. *Education Policy Analysis Archives, 24*(58), 1-27.

Appiah, A. (2006). *Cosmopolitanism: Ethics in a world of strangers.* New York: W. W. Norton & Co.

Appiah, K. A. (2008). Education for global citizenship. In D. Coulter, G. Fenstermacher, & J. R. Wiens (Eds). *Yearbook of the National Society for the Study of Education.* The National Society for the Study of Education. Vol. 1.

Apple, M. W. (1990). *Ideology and curriculum.* New York: Routledge.

Baildon, M., Sim, J. B. Y., & Paculdar, A. (2014). A tale of two countries: Comparing civic education in the Philippines and Singapore. *Compare: A Journal of Comparative and International Education, 46*(1), 93-115.

Banks, J. A. (2008). Diversity, group identity, and citizenship education in a global age. *Educational Researcher, 37*(3), 129-139.

Boggs, G. L. (1998). *Living for change: An autobiography.* Minneapolis: University of Minnesota Press.

Brown, G. W., & Held, D. (2010). *The cosmopolitanism reader.* Cambridge, UK: Polity.

Cogan, J. (1997). *Multidimensional citizenship: Educational policy for the 21st century.* Tokyo: Sasakawa Peace Foundation.

Daipi, H. (2002). Speech by Mr Hawazi Bin Daipi, Parliamentary Secretary (Education): "Globalisation and its impact on social cohesion and rootedness," 5 November at North Zone NE Seminar at Evergreen Secondary School. Retrieved from http://www.moe.gov.sg/media/speeches/2002/sp05112002.htm

Davies, B., & Bansel, P. (2007). Neoliberalism and education. *International Journal of Qualitative Studies in Education, 20*(3), 247-259.

Eisner, E. W. (2002). *The educational imagination: On the design and evaluation of school programs.* Upper Saddle River, NJ: Prentice Hall.

Foucault, M. (1980). *Power/Knowledge.* New York: Random House.

Gaudelli, W. (2009). Heuristics of global citizenship discourses towards curriculum enhancement. *Journal of Curriculum Theorizing, 25*(1), 68-85.

Gaudelli, W. (2010). Seeking a curricular soul: Moving global education into space/place, with intimacy and toward aesthetic experience. *Critical global perspectives: Rethinking knowledge about global societies,* 143-160.

Gaudelli, W., & Heilman, E. (2009). Reconceptualizing geography as democratic global citizenship education. *Teachers College Record, 111*(11), 2647-2677.

GlobeScan. (2016). Global citizenship: A growing sentiment among citizens in emerging economies. Poll commissioned by the British Broadcasting Corporation. Retrieved from http://www.globescan.com/news-and-analysis/press-releases/press-releases-2016/383- global-citizenship-a-growing-sentiment-among-citizens-of-emerging-economies-global-poll.html

Gopinathan, S. (2007). Globalisation, the Singapore developmental state and education policy: A thesis revisited. *Globalisation, Societies and Education, 5*(1), 53-70. http://dx.doi.org/10.1080/14767720601133405

Hahn, C. L. & Alviar-Martin, T. (2008). International political socialization research. In L. Levstik & C. Tyson (Eds.), *Handbook of Social Studies Research,* pp. 81-108. New York, NY: Routledge.

Hanvey, R. (1976). *An attainable global perspective.* New York: Global Perspectives in Education.

Heater, D. B. (2002). *World citizenship: Cosmopolitan thinking and its opponents.* London: Continuum.

Hicks, D. (2003). Thirty years of global education: A reminder of key principles and precedents. *Educational Review, 55*(3), 265-275.

Hirata, J. (2004). Putting gross national happiness in the service of good development. In K. Ura & K. Galay (Eds.), *Gross national happiness and development* (pp. 706-731). Thimphu: The Centre for Bhutan Studies.

Ho, L. C. (2012). Sorting citizens: Differentiated citizenship education in Singapore. *Journal of Curriculum Studies, 44*(3), 403-428.

Ho, L., Alviar-Martin, T., & Leviste, E. (2014). There is space and there are limits: The challenge of teaching controversial topics in an illberal democracy. *Teachers College Record, 116*(5), 1-28.

Ho, L., Alviar-Martin, T., Sim, J., & Yap, P. (2011). Civic disparities: Exploring students' perceptions of citizenship within Singapore's academic tracks" *Theory and Research in Social Education, 39*(2), 203-237.

Kennedy, K. J., & Fairbrother, G. P. (2004). Asian perspectives on citizenship education in review: Postcolonial constructions or precolonial values. In WO.

Kennedy, K. J., Lee, W. O., & Grossman, D. (Eds.) (2010). *Citizenship pedagogies in Asia and the Pacific.* Dordrecht, NL: Springer.

Lee, W. O., Grossman, D. L., Kennedy, K. J. & Fairbrother, G. P. (Eds.), *Citizenship education in Asia and the Pacific: Concepts and issues* (pp. 289-301). Hong Kong: CERC.

Lee, W. O. (2006). *Tensions and contentions in the development of citizenship curriculum in Asian countries.* Keynote address delivered at the CitizEd International Conference, Oriel College, Oxford, England.

Lee, W. O. (2009). *Conceptualising citizenship and citizenship education: A trajectory of exploring Asian perspectives.* Hong Kong Institute of Education Chair Professors Public Lecture Series, 1, 1-52.

Lokamitra, D. (2004). The centrality of Buddhism and education in developing gross national happiness. In K. Ura & .K Galay (Eds.), *Gross national happiness and development* (pp. 472-482). Thimphu: The Centre for Bhutan Studies.

Martin, J. R. (1994). *Changing the educational landscape: Philosophy, women, and curriculum.* NY: Routledge.

Ministry of Education (MOE, Singapore). (2000). The 2000 Report of the Committee on Compulsory Education in Singapore, July 2000. Retrieved from http://www.moe.gov.sg/initiatives/compulsory-education/files/ce-report.pdf

Ministry of Education (Singapore). (2008). Combined Humanities Ordinary Level Social Studies (Syllabus 2192). Retrieved from https://www.seab.gov.sg/content/syllabus/olevel/2014Syllabus/2192_2014.pdf

Ministry of Education, Culture, Sports, Science and Technology. (2003). White paper on science and technology. Tokyo: MEXT. Retrieved from http://www.mext.go.jp/b_menu/hakusho/html/hpag200301/hpag200301_2_019.html

Ministry of Education, Culture, Sports, Science and Technology. (2006). The revisions of the courses of study for elementary and secondary schools. Tokyo: MEXT. Retrieved from http://www.mext.go.jp/english/elsec/__icsFiles/afieldfile/2011/03/28/1303755001.pdf

Ministry of Education, Culture, Sports, Science and Technology, Japan. (2008) *The Basic Plan Basic for the Promotion of Education.* Tokyo: MEXT. Retrieved from:

Ministry of Education, Culture, Sports, Science and Technology, Japan. (2013a) *The Second Basic Plan for the Promotion of Education.* Tokyo: MEXT. Retrieved from: http://www.mext.go.jp/english/lawandplan/1355330.htm

Ministry of Education, Culture, Sports, Science and Technology, Japan. (2013b). *Revisions of the Courses of Study.* Tokyo: MEXT. Retrieved from http://www.mext.go.jp/english/elsec/__icsFiles/afieldfile/2011/03/28/1303755_001.pdf

Mitchell, K. (2003). Educating the national citizen in neoliberal times: From the multicultural self to the strategic cosmopolitan. *Transactions of the Institute of British Geographers, 28*(4), 387-403. http://dx.doi.org/10.1111/j.0020-2754.2003.00100.x

Myers, J. P. (2016). Charting a democratic course for global citizenship education: Research directions and current challenges. *Education Policy Analysis Archives, 24*(55), 1-16.

Noddings, N. (2005). "Global citizenship: Promises and problems." In N. Noddings (Ed.), *Educating citizens for global awareness* (pp. 1-11). New York: Teachers College Press.

Nussbaum, M. C. (2010). *Not for profit: Why democracy needs the humanities.* Princeton, NJ: Princeton University Press.

Nussbaum, M. C. (2012). *The new religious intolerance: Overcoming the politics of fear in an anxious age.* Cambridge, MA: Harvard University Press.

Ong, A. (1999). *Flexible citizenship: The cultural logics of transnationality.* Durham, NC: Duke University Press.

Ong, A. (2006). "Experiments with freedom: Milieus of the human." *American Literary History*, 18(2), 229-244.

Osler, A., & Starkey, H. (2005). *Changing citizenship: Democracy and inclusion in education.* Berkshire, UK: Open University Press.

Otsu, K. (2008). Citizenship education curriculum in Japan. In D. L. Grossman, W. O. Lee, & K. J. Kennedy (Eds.), *Citizenship curriculum in Asia and the Pacific.* Dordrecht, NL: Springer

Oxley, L., & Morris, P. (2013). Global citizenship: A typology for distinguishing its multiple conceptions. *British Journal of Educational Studies, 61*(3), 301-325. http://dx.doi.org/10.1080/00071005.2013.798393

Parker, W. (2011). 'International education' in US public schools. *Globalisation, Societies and Education*, 9(3-4), 487-501. http://dx.doi.org/10.1080/14767724.2011.605330

Reid, W. A. (2003). Curriculum as institutionalized learning: Implications for theory and research. *Journal of Curriculum and Supervision, 19*(1), 29-43.

Royal Government of Bhutan. Ministry of Education. Department of Curriculum Research and Development. (2011). *Educating for GNH. Refining Our School Education Practices: A Guide to Advancing Gross National Happiness.* Paro: Author.

Sakurai, R. (2011). Preserving national identity and fostering happiness in an era of globalization: A comparative exploration of values and moral education in Bhutan and Japan. *Journal of International Cooperation Education, 14*(2), 169 -188.

Sassen, S. (2014). *Expulsions: Brutality and complexity in the global economy.* Cambridge, MA: Harvard University Press. http://dx.doi.org/10.4159/9780674369818

Sen, A. (2010). *The idea of justice.* Cambridge, MA: Harvard University Press.

Spring, J. H. (2004). *The intersection of cultures: Multicultural education in the United States and the global economy.* Boston: McGraw-Hill.

Steiner-Khamsi, G. (2010). The Politics and Economics of Comparison. *Comparative Education Review, 54*(3), 323-342.

Torney-Purta, J., Lehmann, R., Oswald, H., & Schulz, W. (2001). *Citizenship and education in twenty-eight countries: Civic knowledge and engagement at age fourteen.* Amsterdam: IEA.

UNESCO. (2013). *Regional report on transversal competencies in education policy and practice.* Bangkok: UNESCO.

UNESCO. (2014). *Global citizenship education: Preparing learners for the challenges of the 21st century.* Paris: UNESCO.

United Nations News Center. (2012). Interview with Prime Minister of Bhutan, Jigmi Y. Thinley. Retrieved from http://www.un.org/apps/news/newsmakers.asp?NewsID=49

Wangyal, T. (2001). Ensuring Social Sustainability: Can Bhutan's Education System Ensure Intergenerational Transmission of Values? *Journal of Bhutan Studies*, 3(1), 106-31. Retrieved from http://www.thlib.org/static/reprints/jbs/JBS_03_01_04.pdf

Yoshimura, K. (2011). The characteristics of citizenship education practices in Japan: Two projects that teach controversial issues. In N. Ikeno (Ed.), *Citizenship education in Japan* (pp. 95-106). London: Continuum.

Zam, D. (2008). *Development of education: National report of Bhutan.* Retrieved from:http://www.ibe.unesco.org/National_Reports/ICE_2008/bhutan_NR08.pdf

Zong, G., Wilson, A., & Quashiga, Y. (2008). Global education. In L. Levstik & C. Tyson. (Eds.), *Handbook of Social Studies Research* (pp. 197-216). NY: Routledge.

*

Lukas S. Ispandriarno
Martin Löffelholz

Internationalizing Higher Education in Indonesia

FOR A MAJORITY of Indonesia's younger generation, gaining access to higher education promises a pathway for a better future. Within two decades, the number of students has quadrupled to approximately six million creating one of the largest tertiary education systems in the world. Undoubtedly, the country has made progress in higher education since the 1997-98 Asian crisis. However, the highly diversified system is still not offering equity access and is often criticized for its lack of quality. At the same time, the growth of Indonesia's trade and industry, its further integration into the global economy, and particularly the rise of the ASEAN Economic Community demand the further expansion, quality enhancement, and internationalization of tertiary education.

Against this background, we analyze how Indonesia's cultural diversity, emerging democracy, and vibrant economy challenge its higher education system in the early 21st century (section 1). Subsequently, we describe to what extent the complex system of tertiary education meets common quality standards (section 2) and how Indonesian higher education institutions are responding to internationalization to improve their competitiveness in the era of globalization (section 3).

The chapter concludes by discussing recommendations on enhancing the competitiveness of higher education in Indonesia.[1]

Cultural diversity, emerging democracy, and vibrant economy

Indonesia is the largest archipelago in the world extending more than 5,100 kilometers from east to west and almost 1,900 kilometers from north to south. It consists of about 17,500 islands and has the world's fourth largest population. According to the UN, approximately 258 million people live in Indonesia (United Nations 2015: 15). The population is relatively young and growing moderately. Both the size of the country and the size and demographic composition of the population cause enormous challenges to primary, secondary, and tertiary education. Likewise, the immense ethnic, cultural, and religious diversity poses a further challenge to (higher) education.

Constitutionally, Indonesia is a country of many religions; however, the vast majority of Indonesians adhere to various forms of Islam. The country comprises more than 300 ethnic groups speaking more than 700 languages (Ethnologue 2017). In 1945, Indonesia's first president, Sukarno, established Indonesian, locally known as Bahasa Indonesia, as the unifying national language. Bahasa Indonesia, a variant of Malay, is widely used in administration, commerce, and education. Nevertheless, many Indonesians still speak other local languages as their first language, such as Javanese, Sundanese, or Balinese (OECD 2015: 55) and some ethnic groups have raised concerns about the teaching of local languages left out of the educational sector diminishing Indonesia's cultural diversity (cf. Suryanto 2013).

History as context

Politically and socio-economically, the Indonesian nation had to cope with severe crises before and after the proclamation of independence on August 17, 1945. With the exception of a short period of British rule, the Dutch controlled Indonesia ("spice trade") until the mid-20th century (Taylor 2003: 238-385). Although the Dutch colonial

1 For their invaluable inputs, the authors are grateful to Mira Rochyadi-Reetz and Kadek Dwi Cahaya Putra, doctorate students at Technische Universität Ilmenau (Germany).

government established a number of universities and colleges on the island of Java, especially the Bandung Institute of Technology in 1920, there was a clear segregation between the Indonesians and the Dutch. This separation ended in 1949 after years of fierce fighting, when the Netherlands withdrew from the archipelago and the United Nations acknowledged Indonesia's independence. Nevertheless, most of the universities founded by the Dutch in the early 20th century had become the country's top educational institutions as of today.

The Japanese occupied the country during the Second World War from 1942 to 1945. Upon Japan's surrender, Indonesian nationalists, Sukarno and Mohammad Hatta, declared independence. However, Sukarno's "guided democracy" ended in a particularly dark period of Indonesian history. After a controversial coup attempt in 1965, large-scale killings occurred, targeting communist sympathizers, ethnic Chinese, and the political left, mostly at the instigation of the armed forces. As a result, the authoritarian "New Order" regime under Suharto "gave technocrats room to run the economy with considerable success, quadrupling per capita income and significantly reducing poverty" (OECD 2015: 54). Yet, the coup attempt and its brutal defeat had badly damaged Indonesia's reputation, prompting it to look for partners within the region to improve its image. In 1967, Indonesia became a founding member of the Association of South East Asian Nations (ASEAN), which gradually developed into a major pillar of Indonesia's foreign policy (Weatherbee 2013).

From 1967 until 1998, Suharto and his cronies ruled Indonesia (Taylor 2003: 356-385). His policy of "allowing army involvement at all levels of government, from top-level state-owned enterprises down to village level fostered corruption, however, and his 'transmigration' programs—which moved large numbers of landless farmers from Java to other parts of the country—fanned ethnic conflict" (OECD 2015: 54). Upon Suharto's forced resignation in May 1998, following the severe Asian financial crisis of 1997-98, Indonesia began a transition to a democratic order.

Indonesia today

The country is now emerging as a vibrant republic, shaped by democratic principles, cultural and religious traditions, and the founder's ideas of "*pañca sila*" (five principles), namely belief in god, just humanity, national unity, democracy based on deliberation, and social justice. Steady improvements in Indonesia's electoral processes since 1998 indicate a stabilization of democracy despite persistent obstacles, i.e. vote buying or corruption. Indonesia's overall successful democratic performance is acknowledged both internationally and by the electorate itself (cf. Mujani and Liddle 2015).

Concurrently, the relevance of Indonesia's economy is steadily increasing. Nowadays, the World Bank (WB) classifies Indonesia as an emerging low middle-income country and lists it as the world's 16th largest economy in terms of gross domestic product (World Bank 2017b). Despite regional socio-economic disparities, it has made gains in poverty reduction, "cutting the poverty rate to more than half since 1999, to almost 11 percent in 2016" (World Bank 2017a). Challenges stem from the ongoing regionalization and internationalization of Indonesia's economy, particularly since the ASEAN Economic Community (heading towards a globally competitive single market and production base) entered into force in late 2015 (Dosch 2016: 100-146). The anticipated free flow of labor and investments may specially challenge Indonesia's rather protectionist tertiary education system.

Moreover, the country still struggles with weak infrastructure and fragile institutions (Asian Century Institute 2016; Tan et al. 2013), widespread corruption (Koenen 2009), increasing religious and ethnic intolerance (Fealy 2017), and other obstacles. Consequently, the global competitiveness index, compiled by the World Economic Forum, ranks Indonesia just 108th out of 138 countries in health and primary education, 100th in labor market efficiency, 91st in technological readiness, 63rd in higher education, and 60th in infrastructure. Overall, Indonesia takes the 41st place, especially due to its market size (cf. Schwab 2016: XIII).

The rapid growth of the economy and the process of democratization in conjunction with wider political and economic freedom correspond to the enlargement of the higher education sector. The number of tertiary education institutions more than quadrupled from 900 by 1990 to more than 3,800 by 2012. Simultaneously, the number of students increased from 1.5 million to approximately 6 million (OECD 2015: 188). While enhancing the quality of higher education is vital for Indonesia's competitiveness, a "key question is whether the tertiary education system as a whole has been able to absorb this massive increase without an erosion of quality" (OECD 2015: 188). In conclusion, Indonesia's economic progress, the rise of the ASEAN Economic Community, and Indonesia's growing relevance as a regional power and member of the G-20 countries demand further expansion and internationalization of tertiary education despite continuing obstacles.

Complexity and quality of higher education in Indonesia

Indonesia's tertiary education structure is highly diversified due to different types of institutions, public and private governance, and the distinction between general and religious education. This enormous complexity results in uncertainty regarding the numbers of higher education institutions. The most recent list compiled by the Ministry of Research, Technology, and Higher Education ("Kementerian Riset Teknologi Dan Pendidikan Tinggi") includes 3,320 institutions (cf. Ministry 2016).

The Organization for Economic Cooperation and Development (OECD) refers to 3,834 universities, colleges, institutes, polytechnics, and academies. Accordingly, there are 3,093 private and 645 Islamic institutions, yet just 95 public universities, colleges, and institutes (see table 1). The Ministry of Research, Technology, and Higher Education (MRTHE) is responsible for general tertiary education and the Ministry of Religious Affairs (MRA) is in charge of Islamic institutions. Additionally, there are about 80 higher education institutes under the responsibility of other ministries ensuring the supply of human resources for their respective institutions (OECD 2015, 185-187).

Table 1
Institutions of higher education in Indonesia

	Universi-ties	Institutes	Colleges	Polytech-nics	Acade-mies	Total
Public	51	7	1	-	36	95
Private	424	51	1383	1099	136	3093
Islamic*	99	44	502	-	-	645
Open	1	-	-	-	-	1
Total	575	102	1886	1099	172	3834

Source: OECD 2015, 187, citing MOEC Higher Education Statistics 2012/2013;
**MORA Islamic Education Statistics 2011/2012*

As stated by the OECD, there are huge differences between the public and private sectors regarding student intake, infrastructure, staff qualification, teaching quality, and extent of internationalization (cf. OECD 2015: 38). According to the assessment by the Ministry of Research, Technology, and Higher Education, no private institution but 11 public universities form the so-called cluster 1 of the national ranking system. The clustering is based on evaluating four dimensions of higher education institutions' performance, namely human resources, management, students, and research and publications.

Public universities, in particular, the Institut Teknologi Bandung, Universitas Gadjah Mada, Institut Pertanian Bogor, and Universitas Indonesia, are among the leading national institutions of tertiary education (MRTHE 2016). Public institutions of higher education are essentially part of the government bureaucracy with very limited autonomy. Seven stronger public universities, however, received the status of a state-owned legal entity ("Badan Hukum Milik Negara"). These institutions enjoy considerably greater autonomy in the fields of management, financing, staffing, and academic matters. They are directly accountable to the public (OECD 2015: 212). At the same time, however, critical scholars note that this policy has "turned education into a money-making business activity" (Nugroho 2003: 144) even in public universities.

Despite various positive developments in recent years, "no Indonesian university is highly placed among the various rankings of world universities" (OECD 2015: 38). While the recent Times Higher Education ranking confirmed the OECD assertion (THE 2017), the QS World University Rankings places Universitas Indonesia 277th and the Institut Teknologi Bandung 331st in the global classification (cf. QS 2017). Recently, the MRTHE expressed its hope that by 2019 at least five Indonesian universities will have entered the group of the world's best 500 universities (Kementerian Riset dan teknologi dan Direktorat Jenderal Kelembagaan 2017). Most public universities, however, are still "rated fair to middling along with a few, perhaps 20, of the more than 3,000 private universities" (OECD 2015: 38).

Two of the most striking aspects of Indonesia's complex system of tertiary education are its very centralized regulatory system (OECD 2015: 211-213) and the huge number of private institutions ranging from understaffed institutes with fewer than 500 students to successful universities. Among the 55 institutions placed in the second-best cluster of the higher education ranking are 28 private and 27 public universities (see table 2). The intermediate group (cluster 3) includes 644 promising universities and colleges. Nevertheless, the majority – 2,610 mostly private institutions – are ranked low or very low (Ministry 2016). In 2015, the government sent a strong signal blacklisting 243 higher education institutions due to misconduct, such as manipulated graduate certificates, inappropriately qualified lecturers, or improper implementation of courses (Detik.com 2016).

In sum, few private universities offer a competitive quality level of education, whereas "the bulk of the private institutions [...] would be rated poor, and many very poor. Academic teaching staff are underqualified by international standards, and their remuneration rates and conditions are relatively poor. Facilities and equipment are inadequate" (OECD 2015: 38).

The distinction between public and private universities, however, does not entirely explain the gaps in quality among higher education institutions. There is also a difference between universities situated in Java and those in the outer Java regions. Institutions on the island of Java more often receive better accreditation results (Kementerian Riset dan teknologi dan Direktorat Jenderal Kelembagaan 2016).

The largely uncoordinated development of private universities since the 1990s has certainly contributed to the heterogeneous structure and quality of higher education in Indonesia. Undoubtedly, the rapid growth of the private sector enabled cost-effective expansion, giving numerous young people access to the system. However, many institutions do not have the managerial, financial, and academic foundation to offer high quality study programs, not to mention research. Simultaneously, "there is a significant backlog of unaccredited higher education institutions and study programs. This problem jeopardizes the quality of student learning, the job prospects of graduates, and the credibility of Indonesian higher education qualifications" (OECD 2015: 38). Not surprisingly, "many graduates fare poorly in the job market" (OECD 2015: 38).

Table 2

Top-ranked higher education institutions in Indonesia 2016 (66 out of 3,320)

Public institutions (rank)	**Private institutions (rank)**
Institut Teknologi Bandung (1), Universitas Gadjah Mada (2), Institut Pertanian Bogor (3), Universitas Indonesia (4), Institut Teknologi Sepuluh Nopember (5) Universitas Brawijaya (6), Universitas Padjadjaran (7), Universitas Airlangga (8), Universitas Sebelas Maret (9), Universitas Diponegoro (10), Universitas Hasanuddin (11), Universitas Andalas (12), Universitas Negeri Malang (13), Universitas Negeri Yogyakarta (14), Universitas Jenderal Soedirman (16), Universitas Negeri Semarang (17), Politeknik Elektronik Negeri Surabaya (18), Universitas Pendidikan Indonesia (19), Universitas Riau (20), Universitas Negeri Surabaya (21), Universitas Lampung (22), Universitas Sriwijaya (23), Universitas Negeri Medan (29), Universitas Jambi (30), Universitas Negeri Makassar (31), Universitas Tadulako (35), Universitas Mataram (36), Universitas Bengkulu (37), Universitas Sumatera Utara (38), Universitas Jember (45), Universitas Pendidikan Ganesha (46), Universitas Mulawarman (48), Politeknik Negeri Jakarta (49), Institut Seni Indonesia Yogyakarta (50), Universitas Udayana (57), Universitas Lambung Mangkurat (58), Universitas Negeri Jakarta (60), Universitas Syiah Kuala (61)	Universitas Kristen Petra Surabaya (15), Universitas Sanata Dharma Yogyakarta (24), Universitas Katolik Parahyangan (25), Universitas Muhammadiyah Malang (26), Universitas Surabaya (27), Universitas Katolik Widaya Mandala Surabaya (28), Universitas Islam Bandung (32), Universitas Katolik Atma Jaya Jakarta (33), Universitas Muslim Indonesia (34), Universitas Katolik Soegijapranata (39) Universitas Bina Nusantara (40), Universitas Muhammadiyah Surakarta (41), Universitas Islam Malang (42), Universitas Muhammadiyah Yogyakarta (43), Universitas Mahasaraswati Denpasar (44), Universitas Gunadarma (47) Universitas Islam Indonesia (51), Universitas Kristen Maranatha (52), Universitas Muhammadiyah Jakarta (53), Universitas Al-azhar Indonesia (54), Sekolah Tinggi Hukum Bandung (55), Universitas Narotama (56), Universitas Nasional (59) Universitas Pancasila (62), Institut Sains Dan Teknologi Akprind (63), Universitas Kristen Satya Wacana (64), Universitas Wijaya Kusuma Surabaya (65), Universitas Atma Jaya Yogyakarta (66)

Source: Ministry of Research, Technology and Higher Education 2016

Also problematic is that several institutions are under the control of political figures, paternalistic oligarchs, or industry conglomerates. Formally run by not-for-profit foundations (*yayasan*), some private universities contribute rather to commercialization than to education—despite respective legal regulations. According to Law No. 16 of 2001 on Foundations, amended by Law No. 28 of 2004, a *yayasan* is a "non-membership legal entity, established based on the separation of assets, and intended as a vehicle for attaining certain purposes in the social, religious, or humanitarian fields" (Council on Foundations 2016). Foundations must consist of the Governing Board ("Badan Pembina"), Supervisory Board ("Badan Pengawas"), and Executive Board ("Badan Pengurus"). The law requires strict separation among the organs of the foundation and underlying business activities. Particularly, the law does not permit board members to receive salaries or honoraria, nor any return on investment. It is an open secret that some Indonesian oligarchs, politicians, and other individuals abuse the foundation-model pretending to follow social responsibilities, yet in reality violating legal provisions.

Against this background, several Indonesian governments have recognized the need to regulate the private sector and enhance the quality of tertiary education. Law No. 17/2013 makes the supervisory mechanisms of civil society organizations, including *yayasan*, subject to government regulation. The Higher Education Act No. 12/2012 sets the legal framework for further advancements regarding autonomy, quality, access, and internationalization. Generally, the Act aims at providing universities with greater autonomy and making them more accountable for their results. It is a "fairly comprehensive legal basis for higher education development, covering key elements such as institutional autonomy, wider and equitable access, qualification framework, quality assurance system, as well as strengthening of vocational education and training" (Moeliodihardjo n.d.: 4).

As to the equity of access for children of people often excluded from higher education, the law stipulates that in public universities "20% of the students [...] should be drawn from the lowest socio-economic quintile of the population" unlike the current practice of less than 5% of the lowest socio-economic quintile enrollment (World Bank 2014: 2).

The Higher Education Bill also re-emphasizes higher education's three core objectives as described in the National Development Program 1989-1994. Universities and lecturers are obliged to fulfill the "Tri Dharma Perguruan Tinggi," the three principles of higher education, namely education, research, and community service. Article 50 and 90 of the Higher Education Bill refer to international cooperation in general and the role of foreign universities in particular.

Objectives and framework of internationalizing tertiary education in Indonesia

The 2012 law is an attempt to cope with the global reconfiguration of economies, including Southeast Asia's conversion into a single market, by enhancing Indonesia's competitiveness in higher education. In 2014 the MRTHE issued regulations on domestic and international cooperation in higher education (cf. Ministry 2014). The regulations state that university cooperation should aim at "improving the effectiveness, efficiency, productivity, creativity, innovation, quality, and relevance of the implementation of the three responsibilities of higher education to enhance the nation's competitiveness" (Ministry 2014). Building on the provisions of the 2012 law and the 2014 regulations, Indonesia's approach to internationalizing higher education is largely in line with objectives discussed in the academic discourse.

Scholars define internationalization as "both a response to globalization and a causal force hastening its further development" (Mitchell and Nielsen 2012: 12). It is an "intentional process of integrating an international, intercultural, or global dimension into the purpose, functions, and delivery of post-secondary education, in order to enhance the quality of education and research for all students and staff, and to make a meaningful contribution to society" (De Wit 2015). Integrating internationalization into tertiary education "means developing the culture, attitudes, and practices that enable international and cross-cultural perspectives and approaches to permeate all aspects of university life." (Jones 2013: 162) Comprehensive internationalization is a "commitment, confirmed through action, to infuse international and comparative perspectives throughout the teaching, research, and service missions of higher education" (Hudzik 2011: 1).

Table 3
The internationalization of higher education: normative dimensions

Defined as an intentional process and self-commitment confirmed through action;
Refers to global, international, cross-cultural, and comparative aspects of higher education;
Affects the entire university, namely governance, management, teaching, research, service;
Affects purpose, functions, structures, culture, attitudes, and practices of higher education;
Aims at enhancing the competitiveness and quality of education and research;
Intends to make a meaningful contribution to society;
Has to be initiated, developed, and maintained by top-down and bottom-up mechanisms

Source: De Wit 2015, Jones 2013, Hudzik 2011

Comprehensive internationalization affects leadership and governance, faculty and students, service units as well as the institution's external frames of reference, partnerships, and relations (cf. Hudzik 2011). Internationalization should result in an enhanced global standing for Indonesia's tertiary education system, specifically in "increased quality and efficiency of the universities and their outcomes, put Indonesia in the global map of the higher education, research and innovation, stimulate and catalyze the socioeconomic growth, and promote Indonesia in all aspects globally" (Irandoust 2014). In practical terms, universities and colleges successfully "internationalize" when they "reshape their purposes to attract international students, deploy their programs across national borders, concentrate on internationally advantageous educational program niches, and restructure work roles or compensation systems to recruit, retain or manage employees, etc." (Mitchell and Nielsen 2012: 10).

The far-reaching expectations of experts and lawmakers set the frame of reference for assessing the quality of efforts to internationalize higher education in Indonesia. Indeed, the country has made some progress in tertiary education since the 1997-98 Asian crisis. Not surprisingly however, the extent of internationalization still lags compared with OECD averages as well as with some of Indonesia's neighbors.

Among the approximately 3,800 institutions of higher education, few have established adequate international links, carried out an international benchmarking and accreditation, or recruited foreign scholars. (It is indeed quite difficult for foreign academics to teach permanently in Indonesian universities due to restrictive employment and visa regulations).

The 2012 law and the 2014 regulations indicate that Indonesia permits international cooperation under restrictive conditions only, especially as regards operations of foreign universities and the hiring of foreign scholars. According to a British analyst, Indonesia "remains reluctant to open up to the rest of the world, maintaining a protectionist attitude that is holding back its universities and its economy. [...] Indonesia's colleges and universities are protected from foreign competition because the government assumes they are too weak to stand on their own" (Pincus 2015). Unlike Singapore or Malaysia, which explicitly invited external partner institutions, foreign universities intending to operate in Indonesia must work in partnership with an Indonesian university, have a non-profit orientation, prioritize the appointment of Indonesian staff, and support Indonesia's national interest (Higher Education Act 12/2012, Article 90).

As of 2014, annually, about 0.8% of Indonesian higher education students study abroad, compared with 6.1% for Malaysia or 1.9% for Vietnam. Indonesia's inbound mobility rate amounts to 0.1%, compared with 3.3% for Malaysia, 0.5% for Thailand, and 0.2% for Vietnam. The top five destinations for Indonesian students are Australia (10,500), United States (7,500), Malaysia (4,500), Germany (1,700), and Japan (1,500) (Irandoust 2014). For short-term mobility programs such as summer school or students' exchange programs, there is also limited financial support from the government. This primarily affects students from less wealthy families, often studying in regions outside Java or at public universities. In addition to the low level of student mobility, there are "only a few instances of internationalization in curriculum development, benchmarking, cooperative degree programs (such as twinning arrangements and joint or double degrees), and structured student and staff mobility programs" (OECD 2015: 215).

Despite these obstacles, the OECD observed in the ministry and at universities a "strong awareness of the importance of internationalization. There are many initiatives to support and stimulate international networking and collaborative research projects, e.g. the ASEAN research clusters (among others, one on energy, environment, and biodiversity), international PhD grants (e.g. for upgrading university lecturers, involving several countries), and support for attending international seminars" (OECD 2015: 203). These initiatives focus on increasing Indonesia's presence in the international knowledge system as well as its role in regional setups such as the ASEAN Universities Network (cf. Welch 2012).

In 2010, the government launched a capacity-building program strengthening the offices of international affairs of universities regarding the management of international relations, international student support activities, and international outreach management. As of 2015, 116 universities received grants under this program, indicating a strong interest in developing international relations (*Kementerian Riset dan teknologi dan Direktorat Jenderal Kelembagaan* 2016). The OECD hopes that these positive trends will be given "further impetus not least through active, concrete bilateral agreements with other countries and between higher education institutions" (OECD 2015: 203).

Given Indonesia's socio-economic and regional divergences and considering the heterogeneity of higher education institutions, it is neither likely nor compulsory that all of them engage in internationalization. While most top-tier institutions actively engage in internationalization, the vast majority of universities remain reluctant to adjust to globalization. Despite the efforts of the Indonesian government, missions, student intake, resources, teaching quality, readiness to conduct research, and responsiveness to the labor market differ enormously thus producing diverse responses to the challenges of globalization. To understand how universities respond to these challenges, it is useful to take a deeper look at a specific case, namely the internationalization of Universitas Atma Jaya Yogyakarta, which the authors of this chapter have monitored and participated in for two decades.

University responses to internationalization

The Universitas Atma Jaya Yogyakarta (UAJY) embarked on its path to internationalization in the early 1990s and slowly but steadily became one of the top-ranked higher education institutions in Indonesia (see table 2). Founded on September 27, 1965 as the Atma Jaya Catholic University of Indonesia, Yogyakarta Branch, the university separated from its sister institution in Jakarta in 1973, becoming UAJY. Upon passing government's accreditation in the 1970s, UAJY gradually developed into one of the leading private universities in Indonesia.

Currently, approximately 11,300 students signed up in 11 undergraduate and six graduate study programs, including four programs offering classes using English as the language of instruction. The Indonesian National Accreditation Board of Higher Education (BAN-PT) has accredited all study programs. At present, the university comprises six faculties and employs six professors, 58 scholars with doctorates, 206 with a master's degree, and six with a bachelor's degree. In addition, several well-known part-time lecturers, scholars, and practitioners, some of them with an international background, support teaching and research.

UAJY's name derives from the Sanskrit words *Atma* meaning soul and *Jaya* meaning superior. Hence, from the beginning, the founders of the university were striving for excellence in higher education along with high moral values. Accordingly, UAJY aims to participate in the intellectual life of the nation through global-oriented education. It intends to nurture the academic community carefully and critically in helping to protect and improve the dignity of all human beings and the nation's cultural heritage. These goals guide education and teaching, research and community service, as well as governance and organizational culture. In the early 1990s, the aspiration to offer an excellent education in all study areas motivated the university to establish bilateral relationships with international partners and to begin sending lecturers abroad to pursue higher academic degrees.

In this first phase of internationalization, UAJY's Language Center set up a relationship with Princeton's Asian branch sending native English speakers helping to prepare lecturers to study at various universities in Asia, Australia, Europe, or the USA. Simultaneously, the university, both as an institution as well as lecturers in their individual capacities, began to collaborate with various external partners. Nowadays, UAJY cooperates with 25 higher education institutions in 12 countries and is a member of various higher education associations, especially the Association of Indonesian Catholic Colleges (APTIK). Since APTIK is part of the Association of Southeast and East Asian Catholic Colleges and Universities (ASEACU) and the International Federation of Catholic Universities (IFCU), the membership in APTIK contributes to expanding UAJY's network to the global level.

Another of the early steps towards a more internationalized academic environment commenced when the Department of Communication in the Faculty of Social and Political Sciences invited a German guest professor from the Institute of Media and Communication Science of Technische Universität, Ilmenau (TUI). In 2000 and 2001, Prof. Löffelholz, co-author of this article, spent several months at UAJY, funded by the German Academic Exchange Service (DAAD), guiding UAJY lecturers on research. In 2001, he also accompanied the first group of 15 foreign students from TUI, who visited UAJY to engage in various activities with their Indonesian counterparts.

In the following years, both partners exchanged lecturers and students, visited each other regularly, hosted academic conferences, and published jointly. Three lecturers from UAJY studied several years at Technische Universität Ilmenau earning their doctorate or their master's degree from the German partner institution. Now, two decades later, this cooperation is still ongoing and dynamic due to intensified personal relations, mutual respect, as well as initiatives and interest from both partners.

The second stage of internationalization began in 2009 upon the establishment of the Office of Cooperation and Promotion. Since 2010, this office got support from the Directorate of Higher Education within the program "Strengthening International Affairs Offices." To oversee operations (especially to take care of domestic and international collaborations), the foundation and university appointed an extra vice-rector. Since 2010, the Directorate General of Higher Education also provides more grants for scholars of UAJY to attend international academic conferences.

Thus, the university encourages all lecturers to enter the international sphere by applying for governmental grants to accelerate internationalization and improve UAJY's competitiveness, not least within the ASEAN context.

Since the ASEAN Economic Community became a realistic objective, some UAJY students are more interested in internships or exchange semesters in neighboring countries. The university too has strengthened its cooperation with partners in the ASEAN region, e.g. the De La Salle University in the Philippines. Furthermore, the university supports various initiatives strengthening UAJY's overall internationalization and competitiveness:

- The university-to-university program encourages partner universities, especially members of the aforementioned Catholic associations, to send lecturers interested in teaching at UAJY. This program already attracted scholars from Macquarie University and Murdoch University (Australia), the Embassy of Sweden in Indonesia (Sweden), Swansea University (United Kingdom), and Saint Louis University (Philippines). In the future, the Indian Council for Cultural Relations also intends to support this initiative.
- The Credit Transfer Program, initiated in 2008, aims at harmonizing the conversion of credit points across different higher education systems. Participants are universities from China, Denmark, France, Germany, Japan, Malaysia, the Netherlands, and South Korea.
- The short-course program (workshops on various topics) started in 2013 aims at attracting foreign students to spend some time at UAJY. As of now, students from Technical University Melaka (Malaysia), Technische Universität Ilmenau (Germany), Universität Passau (Germany), Rotterdam Business School (Netherlands), Rotterdam University (Netherlands), Southern Denmark University (Denmark), Universite Catholique de Lille (France), De La Salle University (Philippines), Murdoch University (Australia), University of Puget Sound (USA), and students from Indonesian universities attended the courses.

The previous University Master Plan (2015-2017) also focuses on increasing the number of foreign students. From 2007, the number of foreign students studying in UAJY has increased to as many as 183 young people from 43 countries. Participants come from the Developing Country Partnership Program (KNB), Darmasiswa scholarship programs, credit transfers, and short-term programs. The KNB program started in 2010 encouraging 34 students from 16 countries, whereas the Darmasiswa program attracted 66 students from 23 countries. Furthermore, the student mobility program includes an international community service with De La Salle University (Philippines) and the implementation of a double degree program involving three British partner universities.

There is still a long way to adjust the curriculum of study programs, encourage lecturers and students to prepare for an internationalized environment, and increase the collaboration with the business sector. While the top-down mechanisms of internationalization at UAJY are largely in place, the bottom-up perspective still deserves further attention. The pace and the form of internationalization differ from faculty to faculty and from study program to study program. Several study programs, for instance Management, Accounting, Industrial Engineering, Civil Engineering, Communication Science, or Sociology have already experienced offering classes attended by foreign students. However, not all lecturers are able or willing to teach in English or to add international aspects to their syllabi. The university accepts and respects individual differences since the transformation into an internationally oriented and recognized institution takes time.

Recommendations on enhancing Indonesia's competitiveness in higher education

Indonesia's system of tertiary education is highly diversified and, paradoxically, very centralized as regards the regulatory mechanisms. The quality of study programs and research ranges from fair to very poor, even according to the internal assessment and classification scheme of the MRTHE. The uncoordinated development of the private sector since the 1990s has resulted in a huge number of institutions, some of which obviously deserve neither the label "higher," nor "education." Given this situation, the numerous measures of various Indonesian government entities to enhance the quality and competitiveness of higher education are necessary and mostly beneficial but apparently not yet sufficient.

Table 4

Policy recommendations by World Bank's Core Higher Education Group

Make tertiary education and training more equitable and affordable;
Diversify options while levelling the playing field;
Improve secondary education;
Embrace competition (at national and global levels) in education;
Assure that institutions maintain high quality;
Target public resources toward programs with high (as research users) social returns;
Expand institutional autonomy in exchange for accountability;
Increase the efficiency of institutions, the system, and training providers;
Use innovative approaches to bolster retention and graduation rates;
Give students the information they need to make good decisions about their education

Source: Negara et al. 2014

The World Bank, the Organization for Economic Cooperation and Development, the Asian Development Bank, and other actors support Indonesia in its determination to improve governance, quality, accessibility, and competitiveness of academic learning, research, and services. Enhancing the quality of tertiary education clearly corresponds to improvements in secondary education and an efficient administrative and regulatory system. Financial resources have to be sufficient and effectively utilized. Those universities, which have proven their strength over a certain period, will benefit from greater institutional autonomy in exchange for accountability. In conjunction with these factors, internationalization contributes to an enhanced standing and competitiveness of Indonesia's tertiary education system aiming at an increased quality and efficiency of universities and their outcomes (World Bank 2017a, 2017b, 2014; OECD 2015; Negara et al. 2014).

There is no doubt that Indonesia's economic growth, the rise of the ASEAN Economic Community, and the country's relevance as a regional power demand an improvement of tertiary education in terms of quality, governance, and internationalization. Internationalizing teaching, research, and services not only benefit the economy but give students and scholars alike the "chance to share cultural differences or personal similarities by studying in the same academic fields," (Mitchell and Nielsen 2012: 12) contributing to an enhanced understanding of other cultures and people. It is very visible that many actors in Indonesia—from politicians to industry captains, from researchers to undergraduate students—are increasingly keen to experience the world and simultaneously share their Indonesian cultural roots and traditions with this world.

We would like to conclude this chapter by quoting professor emerita Elspeth Jones, who compiled a list of five key messages on how to implement internationalization successfully into a university's mission and structure:

- The rationale and purpose for internationalization needs to be supported by senior leaders and articulated clearly as a context for the institution's international engagement. [...]
- Internationalization is for all staff, whether in teaching, research, senior administration, or support roles. [...]
- Embed staff development for internationalization into review, recognition, and reward processes for academic and professional support staff to make it clear that such engagement is valued. [...]
- Resources need to follow commitment to internationalization, whether for staff development, overseas initiatives, or to support curriculum internationalization for all; consideration needs to be given to appropriate funding and staffing resources. [...]
- Monitor, evaluate, and review" (Jones 2013: 177).

References

Asian Century Institute. (2016, April 6). *Indonesia's infrastructure crisis*. Retrieved from http://asiancenturyinstitute.com/development/1111-indonesia-s-infrastructure-crisis

Council on Foundations. (2016). *Indonesia*. Retrieved from https://www.cof.org/content/indonesia

Detik.com. (2016). *Ini daftar 234 kampus yang di nonaktifkan kemenristek dikti.* Retrieved from https://news.detik.com/berita/3033481/ini-daftar-243-kampus-yang-dinonaktifkan-kemenristek-dikti.

De Wit, H. (2015). *Quality assurance and internationalization: Trends, challenges and opportunities.* Chicago: INQAAHE.

Dosch, J. (2016). *Die ASEAN-Wirtschaftsgemeinschaft.* Überblick für Wissenschaft und Praxis [The ASEAN Economic Community. Overview for Science and Practice]. Baden-Baden: Nomos.

Ethnologue. (2017). *Languages of the world: Indonesia.* Retrieved from https://www.ethnologue.com/country/ID

Fealy, G. (2017). Bigger than Ahok: Explaining the 2 December mass rally. *Indonesia at Melbourne.* Retrieved from http://indonesiaatmelbourne.unimelb.edu.au/bigger-thanahok-explaining-jakartas-2-december-mass-rally

Hudzik, J. K. (2011). *Comprehensive internationalization: From concept to action.* Washington, DC: NAFSA.

Irandoust, S. (2014). High time for internationalization of Indonesian higher learning. *Jakarta Post,* January 11, 2014.

Jones, E. (2013). The global reach of universities: Leading and engaging academic and support staff in the internationalisation of higher education. In R. Sugden, M. Valania, & J. R. Wilson (Eds.). *Leadership and cooperation in academia: Reflecting on the roles and responsibilities of university faculty and management.* Cheltenham: Edward Elgar.

Kementerian Riset dan teknologi dan Direktorat Jenderal Kelembagaan. (2016). Target dan Kebijakan Utama. Retrieved from http://stkiptsb.ac.id/download/rakerda2016.pdf.

Kementerian Riset dan teknologi dan Direktorat Jenderal Kelembagaan. (2017). Empat skema pendorong world-class university. Retrieved from http://kelembagaan.ristekdikti.go.id/index.php/2016/04/27/empat-skema-pendorong-world-class-university/

Koenen, S. L. (2009). *Korupsi – Korruption in Indonesien. Einblicke und Hintergründe. [Corruption in Indonesia. Insights and background].* Bremen, Boston: Kellner.

Ministry of Education and Culture of the Republic of Indonesia. (2014). Tentang Kerja Sama Perguruan Tinggi, nomor 14 tahun 2014.

Ministry of Research, Technology and Higher Education [MRTHE]. (2016). Klasifikasi dan pemeringkatan perguruan tinggi Indonesia. Retrieved from http://ristekdikti.go.id/wp-content/uploads/2016/02/klasifikasi20151.pdf

Mitchell, D. E. & Nielsen, S. Y. (2012). Internationalization and globalization in higher education. *InTech.* DOI: http://dx.doi.org/10.5772/48702

Moeliodihardjo, B. Y. (n.y.). Higher education sector in Indonesia. Unpublished manuscript prepared for the international seminar on "Massification of Higher Education in Large Academic Systems." Jakarta: British Council.

Mujani, S. & William Liddle, R. (2015). Indonesia's democratic performance: A popular assessment. *Japanese Journal of Political Science, 16*(2), 210-226. DOI:10.1017/S1468109915000067

Negara, S., Crawford, M., Gao, S., Gann, A, M., Ragatz, A., & Suhartono, G. (2014). *Tertiary education in Indonesia: Directions for policy.* Jakarta: World Bank.

OECD/Asian Development Bank. (2015). *Education in Indonesia: Rising to the challenge.* Paris: OECD. DOI: http://dx.doi.org/10.1787/9789264230750-en

QS (2017). World Universities Rankings. Retrieved from https://www.topuniversities.com/university-rankings

Schwab K. (Ed.) (2016). *The Global Competitiveness Report 2016–2017.* Geneva: World Economic Forum. Retrieved from http://www3.weforum.org/docs/GCR2016-2017/05FullReport/TheGlobalCompetitivenessReport2016-2017_FINAL.pdf

Suryanto. (2013, January 16). Pelajaran bahasa daerah tetap ada. *Antara News.* Retrieved from http://www.antaranews.com/berita/351761/pelajaran-bahasa-daerah-tetap-ada

Tan, K. G., Amri, M., Low, L., & Tan, K. Y. (2013). *Competitiveness analysis and development strategies for 33 Indonesian provinces.* Singapore: WSPC.

Taylor, J. G. (2003). *Indonesia: Peoples and histories.* New Haven, London: Yale University Press.

Times Higher Education (THE). (2017). Helping the world's universities to achieve excellence. Retrieved from https://www.timeshighereducation.com/student/best-universities/best-universities-asia-pacific-region-2017

United Nations. (2015). World Population Prospects: The 2015 Revision, Key Findings and Advance Tables. Working Paper No. ESA/P/WP.241. Retrieved from https://esa.un.org/unpd/wpp/publications/files/key_findings_wpp_2015.pdf

Weatherbee, D. E. (2013). *Indonesia in ASEAN: Vision and reality.* Singapore: ISEAS.

Welch, A. (2012). The limits of regionalism in Indonesian higher education. *Asian Education and Development Studies, 1*(1), 24-42. DOI: 10.1108/20463161211194441

World Bank. (2014). Equity, access and success in higher education human development sector (Policy brief). Jakarta: World Bank.

World Bank (2017a). The World Bank in Indonesia: Having maintained political stability, Indonesia is one of Asia Pacific's most vibrant democracies and is emerging as a confident middle-income country. Retrieved from http://www.worldbank.org/en/country/indonesia/overview

World Bank (2017b). World Development Indicators database, 17 April 2017. Retrieved from http://databank.worldbank.org/data/download/GDP.pdf

*

Jozon A. Lorenzana
Nida P. Rodriguez

Research Collaboration and Mentoring at a Distance

Collaborative Practices, Use of New Media and Relations among Filipino Researchers

THE UNEVEN QUALITY of education in the Philippines is not only attributed to regional economic disparities (Mesa 2007) but also to geographical locations of provinces and their peace and order situations. These factors tend to exclude educational institutions in these places from opportunities, which presently are concentrated in the metropolis (Symaco 2013a). Two regions in the southern island of Mindanao, among others, illustrate this situation: the Autonomous Region of Muslim Mindanao (ARMM) and the Caraga Administrative Region (Caraga). ARMM is in the central part of the island comprising the provinces/islands of Basilan, Lanao del Sur, Maguindanao, Sulu, and Tawi-Tawi. Caraga is a grouping of five provinces/islands in the northeast part of Mindanao, namely: Agusan del Norte, Agusan del Sur, Surigao del Norte, Surigao del Sur, and Dinagat Islands. Both regions are distant from metropolitan areas. Unlike the Caraga region, ARMM has been marred by decades of armed conflict between the government and terror groups or entities seeking autonomy from the Philippine state. The five-month siege of Marawi City in Lanao del Sur by ISIS-affiliated groups in 2017 reinforces the perception of instability in the region.

Recent statistics from the Commission on Higher Education (CHED), the regulatory body for tertiary education in the Philippines, indicate the disadvantaged position of the two regions. Compared to the number of private (317)/public (28) higher education institutions (HEIs) in the National Capital Region (NCR), where the capital city Manila is located, ARMM has only 54 private and 11 public HEIs while Caraga has 36 private and 7 public HEIs (Commission on Higher Education [CHED] 2017a). Out of the 18 regions in the country, ARMM (810) and Caraga (752) rank 17th and 18th, respectively, in terms of distribution of higher education programs in academic year 2016-17. They also ranked 17th and 18th for the number of higher education faculty by region (CHED 2017b). While NCR has 32,606 HEI teachers, ARMM and Caraga have 3,131 and 2,989, respectively. In relation to urban centers in Mindanao, both ARMM and Caraga have fewer compared to Davao region with 6,404 HEI teachers (CHED 2017b).

Neoliberal reforms in higher education aimed at making institutions competitive, such as standardization and quality assurance systems, only heighten the situation of inequality. Institutions that lack access to resources and competencies are at a disadvantage. In 2012, CHED issued a policy standard that aimed at implementing "a learning outcomes-based quality assurance framework differentiated by type of higher education institution" (CHED 2012). The policy seeks to make higher education institutions more focused in their efforts to provide quality education based on their area of expertise, resources and relevance to communities or publics that they serve.[1] Since 2011, CHED has closed down 358 programs across regions for non-compliance with minimum quality standards (CHED 2011; Symaco 2013b). Under recent CHED reforms, higher education institutions in the Philippines, especially in disadvantaged positions, need to find ways to maintain or improve their status.[2]

This article describes how a university based in Cotabato City in the ARMM region, an area distant from metropolitan centers and affected by ongoing conflicts in Mindanao, has responded to neoliberal reforms in Philippine higher education through collaboration and mentoring. This university initiated a research collaboration program with a top university based in Manila. Aside from producing peer-reviewed publications, the project had an informal mentoring component where researchers from the Cotabato university would learn from their Manila collaborators how to develop publishable work.

The Cotabato-based institution is a leading center for knowledge concerning social and political issues in the region; various agencies tap its resources for research, particularly data collection. Thus, while it is located in a disadvantaged region, the university has a relative advantage compared to other HEIs in the ARMM region. However, according to its administrators, the university still needs to develop its capacity to produce refereed publications that the new CHED Quality Assurance framework requires. Through a mentoring program in which researchers from the university in Manila acted as mentors, the Cotabato university hoped to develop its faculty members' research capacity and output. It was able to source funds from its international network to compensate the researchers and provide modest funding for the research projects. In this case, we have a situation where a presumably disadvantaged institution finds the economic resources to enable it to tap more privileged institutions.

Collaboration and mentoring

The conceptual definition of mentoring is contested. Eby, Rhodes, and Allen (2007) highlight the following common attributes of the process: "[Mentoring] is: a unique and dynamic learning partnership between individuals; an asymmetrical yet reciprocal relationship; and a process defined by types of support given by a mentor to a protégé" (Eby, Rhodes, and Allen 2007: 10). Mentoring arrangements can provide professional development and create personal and professional networks (e.g. Hudson 2013; Lorenzana 2015). However, mentoring efforts can be complicated by gender, class and age differences (Ragins and Cotton 1991; Sanchez et al. 2005), and attitudes towards authority (Sedlacek et al. 2007). Thus, mentor-protégé relationships involve tensions that arise from particular backgrounds or dispositions of dyadic partners. At the same time, literature suggest that effective mentoring depends on the quality of relationships between mentor and protégé (Ragins 2007). In this situation, mentoring is a "relationship characterised by high quality connections that enable exchange of resources, personal growth, development of authentic identities and the creation of new knowledge" (Ragins 2007: 291). Using a social capital approach, Ragins emphasizes the character of mentoring as a relationship that enables exchange of resources and networks and provides a safe space for emotional expression (Ragins 2007: 289-90).

Overlapping with the definition of mentoring, collaboration is also a relationship defined by reciprocity, cooperation, and equity (Chan 2015: 112). However, in a critical review of the tropes of collaboration, Chan (2015: 112) points out that collaborative relationships are *also* fraught with tensions attributed to power relations and status differentials between actors. For example, in a research collaboration project in Odisha, India, Lund et al. (2016a) examined relations between the researcher and gatekeeper and found that different access to knowledge and power creates both spaces of inclusion and exclusion among research participants. Although their research project included dialogic research practices, inequality still existed (Lund et al. 2016a: 289-290). Similar to mentoring arrangements, reciprocal relations and interpersonal connection help bridge inequalities in collaborative relations (Lund et al. 2016a; Lund et al. 2016b).

Drawing on these assumptions about mentoring and collaboration, we seek to ascertain the dynamics of relationships formed between Manila- and Cotabato-based researchers (with different capacities and uneven competencies) who participated in the research collaboration project. We ask how collaborators describe their relationship with each other as well as the challenges and constraints that they encountered while doing research at a distance. Taking into account human agency, we investigated how they dealt with tensions and constraints in their mentoring/collaborative relationship. Since use of communication technologies have become instrumental to long-distance collaborations (e.g. Lund et al. 2016b), we also considered how participants used digital media technologies as a means to collaborate and relate with each other. In so doing, our study aims to identify emergent mentoring and collaborative practices and relations that enable/hinder participants to gain research competencies, new knowledge, and connections. To answer these questions, we gathered data through interviews and participant observation with project participants. In the next section, we provide a more detailed description of the project.

The case study: a collaborative project between universities in Cotabato and Manila

The research collaboration project was an initiative of a private-sectarian university based in the City of Cotabato in Maguindanao province. The university is a center of basic and tertiary education in Central Mindanao. Although it has a research institute (affiliated with a religious order) with a reputation for its work on peace and development in the area, research activities are limited to faculty members connected with the institute and the university's research unit where contract projects are housed. Furthermore, these projects are mostly applied research in which faculty members are involved in data collection. The research unit publishes a journal which features the work of faculty members but the publication is yet to be recognized by higher education regulators (i.e. CHED). According to the university's president, only few faculty members actually publish in peer-reviewed national and international journals. However, in order to maintain its status as a university according to government policy, its faculty members must be engaged in peer-reviewed research.

The administration initiated a project to increase research activities in the university by partnering with local and overseas institutions. It received external funding to develop a research collaboration project that aimed to build the research competencies of the university's staff and produce joint publications based on the university's interest in peace, culture and development in Central Mindanao.[3] The strategy was to pair up "junior" researchers from the university with more experienced "senior" researchers from established institutions in the country and overseas who would provide informal research mentoring. One of the assumptions in the design of the collaborative project was to use the Cotabato university's strength in data collection in the locality/region as a springboard to develop its faculty's competency in producing publishable papers through mentoring by published scholars.

Researchers were given small grants and compensation to pursue publishable work, i.e. journal publication. The protégé researchers were given less teaching load in order to have time for the project. Mentors were compensated but did not get time off from their respective institutional commitments. From these mentors' end, participation in the program was a form of outreach. Hence, the program also served to establish connections among participants and between institutions.

The project started at a small scale. The university made an open call for participants in the project. Criteria for selecting participants included their academic ranks, qualifications, and recommendations by immediate superiors. A total of eight participants were selected: half of them were junior faculty members with MA degrees; the other half had PhD degrees and held administrative positions. They were paired with researchers (all with PhD degrees) from universities in Manila, Davao, and Hawaii. The pairing system was based on academic rank and areas of interest. Pairs of collaborators were either of junior and senior rank or of the same rank, i.e. both occupying senior roles in their respective institutions. The external partners were involved because they were part of the university's informal networks. Half of the senior researchers had prior engagements with the university or connections with its officials. Both authors of this article were involved in the project and their task was to document, manage, and examine the research program.

While geographical distance was assumed as one of the conditions of the program, measures were put in place to maintain connection and interaction such as funding for periodic visits of senior researchers, workshops, a conference, and a workroom with Internet access. The project had a timetable of two years (December 2015 - June 2017) with specific milestones, namely: developing the proposal, gathering data, presenting the findings, drafting the paper, and preparing/revising the manuscript for peer review. The pairs of researchers were given a free hand in organizing tasks within the schedule. Each author of the present paper served as group coordinator for the Cotabato-based researchers and Manila-based researchers, respectively. As administrator of the research program, the Cotabato-based author of the paper coordinated with two non-Manila based senior researchers (from Davao and Hawaii). The present study focuses on researchers partnered with Manila-based academics.

The research program started in December 2015 with a two-day workshop in Davao City where junior and senior researchers met for the first time. The initial meeting aimed at building rapport among collaborators, sorting out the proposal, and clarifying their expectations of the project. After this meeting, research activities were conducted at a distance.

Between January 2016 - October 2016, researchers from Manila visited Cotabato to check progress on data gathering and to conduct workshops on research methods. When data were collected and initial findings drafted, junior researchers had the opportunity to present papers with their Manila collaborators. The participation in conferences was a new experience that became an opportunity for Cotabato researchers to present research findings and to meet their mentors in person. Face-to-face meetings enabled them to discuss content of their research and obtain feedback about junior researchers' output and senior researcher's mentoring/research strategy. As part of the requirements of the project, the collaborators presented their findings in a conference organized by the Cotabato university in November 2016. Attended by their peers, officials, and scholars in Mindanao, the conference became a venue to discuss research findings. The remaining months from December 2016 to May 2017 were then devoted to drafting the manuscript for peer review. Data for the study cover only up to this period. In the next section, we identify and discuss the challenges emerging from collaboration at a distance.

Constraints and tensions between participants

From our interviews with the project participants and experience in coordinating and taking part in the research activities, we find material and structural constraints that come in tension with the demands of the research exercise. Realities on the ground such as power cuts that affected online connectivity slowed down research activities of Cotabato researchers. I (co-author from Manila) witnessed during my visit to Cotabato how a sudden power cut hindered the completion of tasks. I was preparing documents for a research workshop when the lights went out. I had to wait for 30 minutes to an hour until power was restored. By then I lost momentum having started to pick up from where I left off. Moreover, power disruptions impeded Internet access which delayed email responses of researchers from Cotabato.

Another constraint that participants identified was the structure and routine of work in their respective universities. In order to devote time for research, Cotabato participants were given six units less from their usual teaching load of 21 units (seven contact hours with students per day) per week. Even with only 15 units or three hours teaching per day of the week, unpredictable demands from students and institutional responsibilities disrupted their work. For example, a researcher with administrative duties shared that urgent matters such as disciplinary action (e.g. students in a brawl) needed immediate attention. Everyday administrative concerns took time away from the project. However, junior participants with no administrative duties were able to do research with their allotted time.

The case of Manila researchers presented a slightly different situation. Compared to the teaching load of Cotabato collaborators, they had 12 units (12 contact hours per week) of teaching in a semester. Half of them had administrative duties. Two out of six mentors had fewer teaching responsibilities due to their status as full professor or part-time faculty. We noticed that among Manila researchers, the two with lighter teaching/no administrative load completed drafts of their paper earlier than their peers. While the mentors had less teaching load compared to their Cotabato colleagues, administrative duties took up time. For example, one mentor shared that she had more time for the research program in its first year. However, when she was appointed research director of a unit in her university, she noted that she had less time to mentor her junior co-researcher. Hence, what the experiences of all participants suggest is that the structure of academic workload in private Philippine universities may not be conducive for research.

Besides material and structural conditions, the lack of competency in scholarly writing emerged as a constraint in the collaboration process. While the project assumed the competency of Cotabato researchers in data collection, it did not anticipate their lack of writing skills for publication. The mentoring aspect of the collaboration was intended to develop their capacity to contribute to the drafting of the manuscript. However, mentors had to address an emergent need to develop skills in scholarly writing (e.g. conceptualizing, presenting, and discussing data). Our interviews suggest that their lack of scholarly writing skills generates a lack of confidence in pursuing tasks. Acknowledging these limitations, project participants initiated ways to address them. In the following section, we discuss emergent collaborative and mentoring practices that were specific to the age combination of researchers.

Emergent collaborative practices and relations among researchers

Studies on mentoring suggest that age differences affect mentoring relations and outcomes (Kram and Isabella 1985; Sedlacek et al. 2007). For instance, in Asian cultures, deference to figures of authority (usually elderly people) tends to characterize the orientation of protégés to their mentors (Sedlacek et al. 2007: 274). We find that particular age combinations resulted in specific relationship dynamics, mentoring approaches, and collaborative practices. Researchers of dissimilar age (young/mature) had a traditional mentoring relationship wherein mentors and protégés had clear expectations of their roles. On the other hand, participants of similar age assumed a peer mentoring arrangement in which they were ambivalent about the role of mentor-protégé in the relationship. These varying relationship dynamics influenced how pairs dealt with the challenges and constraints they encountered in the process of collaborative research. At the same time, our data suggest common patterns in the way participants of the project viewed the experience of collaboration. More than half of the participants reported learning new knowledge from their projects, developing a relationship with their mentor/protégé, and appreciating the value of basic research. In this section, we discuss the mentoring and relationship dynamics that emerged from each type of arrangement.

Between researchers of dissimilar age

Young faculty members from Cotabato experienced a more traditional mentoring relationship with their collaborators. In interviews, they claimed that they accepted their role as learners in the program. Reyna, one of the three young participants, explained: "As junior researchers we are learners. So we expected to do the work." Younger collaborators kept an open mind and deferred to their mentors' research plan. Their projects were more aligned with their mentor's areas of interest. However, their mentors also considered their abilities that could be tapped and honed in the process of doing research.

As mentioned above, one of the challenges of the project was the Cotabato researchers' feelings of inadequacy and reluctance. Jesse, a junior researcher, explained why he felt insecure:

> Like most of us, there was reluctance and hesitation to really pursue it. Firstly, we are not exposed to really doing research. It's also demanding, I mean the expectations are high because the research is for international publication. Our work is mostly teaching fulltime.

Junior researchers' insecurities came from their candid assessment of their lack of ability and the pressure to perform in the project. Mentors took steps to create a more personal relationship with them in which open communication took place. Elena, a senior faculty member from Manila, was paired with Fatima, a junior faculty from Cotabato with a Maguindanaon background. Elena's project required access to local sources which Fatima could facilitate. Initially, the junior researcher felt intimidated: "Fear was there. I told [the university president] I could not do it. Although I have written a master's thesis, the kind of research for journal articles is different. Also, I've been teaching Filipino for the last 16 years. My fear of writing [in English] is there."

Fatima's mentor, Elena addressed her fears by creating an open and friendly space between them.

> In the first few months my sense was there was fear on her part which I appreciated because she expressed it so I felt that to have an imaginative, productive relationship, the first issue to tackle was fear and that's what I attended to in Davao [where the project participants first met]. I did not tell her relax or whatever. I made myself aware to be more relaxed. Not threatening, not self-imposing that was in a way to send the message it's ok, whatever will happen is ok. And it looked like it worked.

Elena shared that they did not focus much on the research work during the start of the project. She initiated interactions where they shared "personal revelations of the self" such as their own "failures and successes."

Their first topic proposal on sultanates in Maguindanao did not push through because they found that no archival sources on the subject existed. Elena had a long-term view of mentoring Fatima and decided to include her in another research project that also dealt with peace and conflict in Mindanao. The new arrangement was also intended to allow Fatima to work with Elena's two graduate students who were of the same age. "So in a way her fear dissipated because we no longer just interact one-on-one. She is now with peers of same age and level. The focus on the dyadic relationship was diffused and shifted to a group relationship. She can now relax," explained Elena. However, she was also aware that her doctoral students were more advanced in research skills and theorizing. Elena did not want to give Fatima a subordinate role just because she was starting off. She divided the work according to the abilities of her researchers. The graduate students took the lead for theorizing, methods, and results. Elena wanted an important role for Fatima and she assigned her the task of interpreting data from Muslim respondents.

Elena expressed a desire for Fatima to be able to carry out a research project on her own. The protégé was not sure if she could become an independent researcher but her mentor assured her that the goal could be achieved gradually. Elena learned about Fatima's ability to write feature essays. With this knowledge, she asked Fatima to draft sections of the paper. Elena worked on her junior researcher's writing by giving feedback on the latter's drafts.

When we interviewed Fatima, she appreciated her mentor's dedication to teach her how to write:

> I also wanted to learn...She asked me about my forte in writing. I said I write feature essays. My mentor thought I'd be good at writing narratives. So she [taught me] how to write narratives for research writing. I appreciated her asking what I can do. Ma'am Elena would give me writing assignments. She asked me to write part of the paper's discussion section. I write and then she would polish it. It's good that there was help [from her graduate students]. She guided me how to write in the style of journal articles. In the process, I saw the difference between research and feature writing.

Indeed, establishing a personal relationship was a step to tap and develop the capacities of research participants to become effective collaborators. This finding is consistent with current literature on collaboration and mentoring (Lund et al. 2016a; Ragins 2007) that suggest how giving importance to interpersonal connection can transform dispositions of actors. The experience of Elena and Fatima also shows how gaps in skills can be bridged through a gradual process of identifying and improving the potential competencies of protégés.

Another mentoring practice that showed a change in a protégé's disposition from insecurity to confidence was a mentor's clear plan of activities. Nenita, a mid-career researcher from Manila, always gave detailed instructions to her junior researcher Jesse. She would always set aside time to check progress of their work through Skype sessions. Jesse shared his experience:

> [I'm] more confident because what and how I am supposed to do and the guidance are clear. Ma'am would also send supplementary materials. When I send a draft, she would ask for a Skype session. She would always initiate a conversation.

Hence, another practice that sustained collaborative work at a distance was frequent communication. We will discuss this aspect of the project in the next section. Like Elena and Fatima, Nenita and Jesse related at a personal level:

> We get along so well. Our communication is very open. And ever since the project started, we had the most conversations. On Easter, she would greet me. I feel it's not just work. Ma'am and I are friends.

Jesse was a young faculty member and planned to embark on doctoral studies. The other two junior researchers were also in the early stages of their academic career. Indeed, we surmise that the traditional mentoring approach works for age dissimilar dyads not only because of the protégés' deference to authority, but also their situation as early career academics who would benefit from the experience of acquiring new skills for their professional development.

Between researchers of similar age

Compared to the more personal relationship between collaborators with age disparities, researchers of similar age and rank in their respective universities tended to have a professional relationship. We analyzed that this mode of relating addressed the ambivalence in the mentoring arrangements of the collaborative project. Anna, a senior researcher from Manila, was paired with Luisa, who had both teaching and administrative duties. The former described a situation in which the mentor-student relation was untenable because her collaborator was not formally her student (i.e. a graduate student) with obligations to fulfil, but actually a colleague in Philippine academia. Thus, expectations between them had to be negotiated in reciprocal and professional terms. Luisa was conscious of her role as a learner in the collaboration; on the other hand, Anna was aware that she could not simply make demands.

In this mode of collaboration between peers, mentors accommodated the research interest of their protégés. Anna's interest in Mindanao focused on intergroup relations; Luisa's research dwelled on educational administration. Considering Luisa's interest, both decided to investigate leadership in multicultural educational organizations. Such a decision enabled both parties to participate effectively. Luisa described her mentor's participative approach:

> Anna's strategy worked. She considered my interest. When we talked first time she asked what my interests were. What did I want? That time I was interested in peace education and educational leadership. [Anna] proposed conflict resolution. But I said I was not exposed to that area. And she said ok what would you like? That was the magic that pushed me through. It was easy for me to write about educational leadership if you are starting with a mentoring relationship. You build on the mentee's interest. For us, considering the mentee's discipline worked. Because you are still teaching [her how to write publishable work]. So it was easier for me to write. But if we worked on conflict resolution, I don't have any exposure there. It would be difficult for me to contribute.

Anna shared that she considered her collaborator's passion. Indeed, thinking of ways to build on interests and competencies of collaborators was a practice that created a sense of ownership of the project.

Work was divided among the participants according to their respective competencies. Anna developed a conceptual framework which she derived from literature in Luisa's field of interest. The latter conducted interviews with respondents and wrote up the results. While administrative assignments disrupted and slowed down their work, both claimed to have been understanding of and accommodating with each other. Pressed for time, intensive mentoring had to be foregone in the latter stages. Anna shared that she had to polish the work herself in order to meet the expected output of the project. While Luisa did not really undergo a thorough mentoring process as experienced by her younger colleagues, she valued her relationship with her mentor.

> She was helpful because I believe in our relationship. The strength of our partnership is because she listens. She immediately understood my interests. I was genuine and honest to tell her, that although I have an Ed.D. (doctorate in education), my exposure is different... I learned that you have to be open. And then exercise interpersonal awareness about how partners work. If you get that feel, there are things that may be avoided in the long run.

Even as both acknowledged that their relationship was not as personal as the rest of the participants, both claimed to have enjoyed a working relationship. Luisa pointed out that her mentor did not make her feel less capable and treated her as equal. Anna also shared that both of them adjusted to each other's situation.

However, our interviews and observations also show the possibility that mentoring can be resisted by collaborators of similar age and academic rank. This situation is complicated by the ambivalence towards mentor-protégé roles, expectations of the project, and the structure/demands of academic work, especially among Cotabato researchers.

Justin, a senior researcher, was paired with Marion, who had extensive experience in applied research. In their case, their expectations of the collaboration diverged. Marion thought that the project only required data collection. Justin, however, expected that his co-researcher would be involved in drafting all parts of the paper. In their initial meetings, they managed to agree on a topic. Since Marion had access to data sources, her responsibility was to put them together. When it was time to write the paper, tension emerged on whose task it was to draft the framework. Marion expected her mentor to provide it; however, Justin thought that his co-researcher as protégé needed to come up with a preliminary analysis of the material in order to ascertain a suitable theoretical framework for their study. Each of them waited for someone to initiate. In our separate conversations with them, we learned that Marion and Justin had different orientations toward research: one theorized in an inductive fashion while the other expected research to have a framework at the start. Compared to Luisa and Anna who adjusted to each other's circumstances and preferences, Marion and Justin could not reach a compromise. Justin thought that his collaborator was free to make a choice in the project. Although they communicated by email, tensions remained until they met face-to-face to clarify expectations. Studies on collaborative relationships in the Asian context (e.g. Chan 2015; Lund 2016a) highlight tensions and complexities. The case of Marion and Justin illustrates the possibility of conflict in collaborative work. In their situation, partners of similar age and rank can *actually* assert themselves compared to age dissimilar dyads where younger partners tend to defer to their senior partners (cf. Sedlacek 2007).

The examples of Anna and Luisa, Justin and Marion present two possibilities when researchers of similar ages collaborate. Our findings suggest that tensions, such as different expectations regarding research practice and disruptions brought about by teaching and administrative responsibilities, can be managed through accommodation and negotiation. Furthermore, we also find that mediation among participants, through organizing mentors and protégés as support groups in themselves, help mitigate tensions. Except for mentors outside Metro Manila, mentors met periodically to exchange experiences and practices. Junior researchers from Cotabato also had regular meetings where they reported on the progress of their work and discussed emerging issues. The meetings were organized by coordinators who updated each other and clarified or explained sentiments and issues raised by the collaborators. Hence, tensions were dealt with through a feedback mechanism mediated by the coordinators. Their mediating role suited the non-confrontational manner in which participants expressed tensions in their relations.

In the next section, we discuss how participants used digital media in dealing with geographical distance.

Role of digital media

Mentoring studies suggest the possibility of connecting at a distance through digital media communications (e.g. Lasater et al. 2013; Lach et al. 2013). Distance itself creates a condition for dyadic partners to be open and vulnerable; however, it is important for partners to have met face-to-face (Lasater et al. 2013: 503-504). At the same time, literature on mediated communication in long distance relationships suggest that access to and use of communication technology reinforce or amplify pre-existing dynamics in a relationship (Madianou and Miller 2012). These assumptions have been validated in our study. We find that digital media platforms such as Skype (video calls), email, and texting helped establish a connection between collaborators and facilitated their work. However, we did not anticipate the impact of power cuts and uneven Internet access on connectivity. Notwithstanding such limitations, researchers from Cotabato found ways to connect with their mentors.

Participants used digital platforms in particular ways. Email was the preferred medium for tasks that required elaborate instructions and exchanging documents. Participants, especially from Cotabato, took time to respond to emails because of unreliable Internet connections at least in the first few months of the project. However, we also found that delayed replies to email messages from their mentors were also caused by their inability to respond to certain queries. Cynthia, a junior faculty member, and Robbie, a senior faculty member, had to figure out the instructions of their mentor, Rosana, before they could reply. The absence of a reply created anxiety and could be interpreted in different ways. Rosana, for example, thought that her junior researchers lacked initiative. The lapse in communication in Rosana's team reflected not so much the unreliability of connectivity but the hesitation of junior researchers. In our interview with Cynthia, we learned that the reason they were unable to reply was their inability to finish the task assigned to them. Cynthia said it was difficult to tell their mentor that they had not done anything yet. However, she also qualified that when they started meeting face-to-face (during Rosana's visits to Cotabato and their participation in two conferences), their understanding of the project and process became clearer. Indeed, face-to-face contact was crucial to the long-distance collaboration. Anxieties and concerns were immediately addressed.

The immediacy of texting (chat applications) made it the most common form of communication among participants. Texting was used for phatic communication and matters requiring immediate attention. They used text in combination with email and Skype. It was also used as a prompt, especially when participants needed to switch to a more engaging means of communication such as voice and video calls. We observed that pairs of young and mature researchers tended to use voice and video calls. For example, Nenita and Jesse would have regular video call sessions where detailed feedback sessions took place. Despite uneven Internet access, younger researchers (who were single or had no administrative roles) found ways to connect. Jesse and Cynthia would go to a neighboring house to get wireless Internet access (WIFI) or a network signal. Interviews with them indicated that they were likely to be happy and satisfied with their mentoring relationship.

Indeed, despite the reality of disruptions in connectivity, digital communications provided a space for collaborators at a distance to interact. As the experiences of our participants show, interpersonal dynamics between junior and senior collaborators were reflected in the way media are utilized. Our data also indicate that misunderstandings due to the long-distance arrangement could be addressed when participants meet face-to-face.

Conclusion and lessons from the project

This chapter explores collaboration and mentoring as a means to bridge gaps between privileged and disadvantaged institutions in the Philippine context. A university in Central Mindanao, a region geographically remote from "centers" of innovation and intellectual activity and also in the crossfires of political conflict, partnered with well-resourced institutions in Manila, Davao, and the US. The project was an ad hoc measure to improve the university's standards and output of research through collaborative research and informal mentoring. Focusing on researchers based in Manila and their respective collaborators from Cotabato, our study sought to identify the challenges and constraints in the program as well as the emergent practices and ways that enabled collaboration and mentoring. The study is premised on the idea that mentoring can facilitate the sharing of knowledge, acquisition of skills, and formation of professional networks (Ragins 2007: 291). Notwithstanding constraints such as material realities, the structure and routine of Philippine academic work, and uneven competencies, researchers from Manila and Cotabato were able to develop collaborative and mentoring relationships that were either professional or personal in nature. We find that age combinations shaped the collaboration/mentoring experience and outcomes: there was less tension in pairs of dissimilar age compared to collaborators of equal age. Younger researchers were more open to the mentoring aspect because it contributed to their professional development. Researchers of similar age and rank tended to assert themselves which potentially generated tensions and conflict. Our finding validates current assumptions that tensions are inevitable in collaborative work (Chan 2015); however, as our study reveals, they can be managed through group mediation or the partners' own initiative.

While the acquisition of research competencies (i.e. writing) was uneven, participants learned about the standards of publishable research. Mentors also gained from the experience through connections they established and the knowledge generated by the exercise. Our study also revealed that although mediated communication enabled connection and facilitated research/mentoring activities, face-to-face communication was crucial in addressing tensions and was a more effective means of instruction.

Although our study is modest in objective and limited in scope, our findings have implications for programs that utilize mentoring and collaboration at a distance: We enumerate them as follows:

1. The program did not have set rules on how mentoring should take place. Collaborators were free to set the terms. Our findings show that, especially for age or rank-similar dyads, the lack of clear expectations on the extent of mentoring and division of tasks become tension points. Hence, in the case of peer mentoring, specific roles

of collaborators/mentor-protégé and learning outcomes need to be identified at the start to ascertain the commitment of participants.

2. While mediated communication can facilitate the accomplishment of tasks even at a distance, it cannot substitute for face-to-face contact. The program allowed for brief face-to-face interactions and relied on mediated communication. We noticed that tasks were more likely to be accomplished face-to-face. Feedback was immediate, therefore it facilitated immediate learning. Thus, mentoring programs at a distance will benefit from face-to-face interactions within reasonable periods, i.e. mentors can alternately dedicate a week of module-based instruction rather than short visits.
3. The study also found that creating support groups enabled participants to share experiences. This activity can also be used as a means to process experiences and concerns of participants and link them to the learning process of gaining research competencies.

Notes

1. The scheme differentiates educational institutions horizontally (based on their type) and vertically (based on their achievement of criteria specific to their category). Types of higher education institutions (HEIs) are determined according to: "qualifications and competencies of their graduates, nature of degree programs offered, qualifications of faculty members, types of available learning resources and support structure, and nature of linkages and outreach" (CHED, 2012, p. 6). CHED identifies three types: professional institutions, colleges, and universities. Vertical assessment of HEIs is based on their alignment of the institution's learning environment with their purpose and function; demonstration of exceptional learning and service outcomes; and a culture of quality (CHED, 2012, p. 9). It results in three assessment categories, namely: autonomous HEIs, deregulated HEIs, and regulated HEIs.

   Outstanding or very good institutional quality and learning outcomes differentiate autonomous from deregulated institutions. The presence of program centers of excellence or development and international accreditation of programs serve as primary indicators of institutional quality. To achieve or maintain a center of excellence/development status, HEIs must demonstrate, among others, a thriving research culture as indicated by refereed publications of faculty members. CHED's recent emphasis on research poses a huge challenge to Philippine HEIs with limited resources, capacity and heavy teaching activities.
2. As part of CHED's efforts to support HEIs in the process of implementing its quality assurance framework, it has created funds to support collaborative work between

universities in the country (CHED, 2011). Hence, the present study examines collaborative efforts among Philippine HEIs.

3. Previous examples of a collective research process involving researchers from Mindanao and Manila include the work of Inzon, Ofreneo and Vela (2013) on everyday violence, peace, and meaning-making in Mindanao. Unlike the present study, Inzon et al.'s (2013) collaborative research did not involve mentoring. Our work draws inspiration from their group-oriented approach where researchers shared their research journey among their peers.

References

Chan, C. (2015). Tensions and complexities in school-university collaboration. *Asia Pacific Journal of Education, 35*(1), 111-124.

Commission on Higher Education. (2011). Highlights of accomplishments: January 2011-December 2011. Commission on Higher Education. Retrieved from http://web.ched.gov.ph/wp-content/uploads/2017/09/FY-2011-CHED-Highlights-of-Accomplishments1.pdf

Commission on Higher Education. (2012). Policy standard to enhance quality assurance (QA) in Philippine higher education through an outcomes-based and typology-based QA. CHED Memorandum Order No. 46. Commission on Higher Education.

Commission on Higher Education. (2017a). Higher education data infographics. Retrieved from http://www.ched.gov.ph/central/page/higher-education-data-infographics

Commission on Higher Education. (2017b). Higher education statistical data. Retrieved from http://www.ched.gov.ph/central/page/ched-statistics

Eby, L. T., Rhodes, J. E., & Allen, T. D. (2007). Definition and evolution of mentoring. In T.D. Allen & L.T. Eby (Eds). *The Blackwell handbook of mentoring: A multiple perspectives approach* (pp. 7-20). Oxford: Wiley-Blackwell.

Hudson, P. (2013). Mentoring as professional development: 'Growth for both' mentor and mentee. *Professional development in education, 39*(5), 771-783.

Inzon, C. M., Ofreneo, M. A. P. & de Vela, T. C. (Eds.) (2013). *Meaning-Making in Mindanao: Everyday violence, ordinary people, finding peace.* Jolo: Notre Dame of Jolo College.

Kram, K. E. (1985). *Mentoring at work: Developmental relationships in organizational life.* Glenview, Illinois: Scott, Foresman and Company.

Kram, K. E., & Isabella, L. A. (1985). Mentoring alternatives: The role of peer relationships in career development. *Academy of management Journal, 28*(1), 110-132.

Lach, H. W., Hertz, J. E., Pomeroy, S. H., Resnick, B., & Buckwalter, K. C. (2013). The challenges and benefits of distance mentoring. *Journal of Professional Nursing, 29*(1), 39-48.

Lasater, K., Young, P. K., Mitchell, C. G., Delahoyde, T. M., Nick, J. M., & Siktberg, L. (2014). Connecting in distance mentoring: Communication practices that work. *Nurse education today, 34*(4), 501-506.

Lorenzana, J. A. (2015). Ethnic moralities and reciprocity: towards an ethic of South-South relations. *Bandung: Journal of the Global South*, *2*(1), 7.

Lund, R., Panda, S. M., & Dhal, M. P. (2016a). Narrating spaces of inclusion and exclusion in research collaboration–researcher-gatekeeper dialogue. *Qualitative Research*, *16*(3), 280-292.

Lund, R., Kusakabe, K., Panda, S. M., & Wang, Y. (2016b). Building knowledge across transnational boundaries: Collaboration and friendship in research. *Emotion, Space and Society*, *20*, 18-24.

Madianou, M., & Miller, D. (2013). *Migration and new media: Transnational families and polymedia*. London: Routledge.

Mesa, E. P. (2007). Measuring education inequality in the Philippines. *Philippine Review of Economics*, *44*(2).

Ragins, B. R., & Cotton, J. L. (1991). Easier said than done: Gender differences in perceived barriers to gaining a mentor. *Academy of Management Journal*, *34*(4), 939-951.

Ragins, B. R. (2007). Diversity and workplace mentoring relationships: A review and positive social capital approach. In T.D. Allen & L.T. Eby (Eds). *The Blackwell handbook of mentoring: A multiple perspectives approach* (pp. 281-300). Oxford: Wiley-Blackwell.

Sanchez, B., Colón-Torres, Y., Feuer, R., Roundfield, K., & Berardi, L. (2005). Race, ethnicity, and culture in mentoring relationships. In D. L. DuBois & M. J. Karcher(Eds). *Handbook of youth mentoring* (pp. 191-204). Los Angeles: Sage.

Sedlacek, W. E., Benjamin, E., Schlosser, L. Z., & Sheu, H. B. (2007). Mentoring in academia: Considerations for diverse populations. In T.D. Allen & L.T. Eby (Eds). *The Blackwell handbook of mentoring: A multiple perspectives approach*, (259-280). Oxford: Wiley-Blackwell.

Symaco, L. P. (2013a). Geographies of social exclusion: education access in the Philippines. *Comparative Education*, *49*(3), 361-373.

Symaco, L. P. (2013b). Education in the knowledge-based society: the case of the Philippines. *Asia Pacific Journal of Education*, *33*(2), 183-196.

*

Alona U. Guevarra

Asian Novels Go Global

Implications in Our Classrooms

GLOBAL LITERATURE is the result of transnational practices in literary production and reception in the age of globalization. Paul Jay defines transnationalism in literary studies as "the *simultaneous* acceleration of globalization and nationalism." For Jay, the early 1990s marked a trend in academe for a transformation to occur within it as "every major field in literary studies [became] transnationalized in its theories, practices and methodologies" (Jay 91). The other force that transformed the discipline of English occurs outside of academia as "English literature (particularly the novel) is being produced by an increasingly transnational, multicultural group of writers, working in disparate parts of the world, whose work explores the intersecting effects of colonialism, decolonization, migration, economic and cultural globalization" (Jay 91). Therefore, what Jay refers to as the transnational turn in literary studies is a product of changes inside and outside the academe. This turn has produced English novels or *novels translated into English,* whose sensibilities are globally accepted, as it "transforms the nature of national literatures" (Jay 92).

Following Jay's observation, the British novelist, translator, and author, Tim Parks, aptly discusses the literary success of a novelist today as such:

> [a] novelist is not famous today unless internationally famous, not recognized unless recognized everywhere. Even the recognition extended to him in his home country is significantly increased if he is recognized abroad. The smaller the country he lives in, the less important his language on the international scene, the more this is the case...The inevitable result is that many writers, consciously or otherwise, have begun to think of their audience as international rather than national. (*The Times Literary Supplement* 2011)

What Parks discusses here is the marked growing consciousness of writing for an international audience by contemporary writers, especially those writers from "smaller countries." By this Parks means small not in size but also in terms of capital. Thus, to write for an international or global audience increases the chance for the writer to receive distinction. What Parks has pointed out describes the current global literary field where translation into a highly-regarded language such as English is of primary importance. What exactly is this global literary field which gave birth to global literature?

What is global literature?

Global literature is transnational literature that crisscrosses boundaries to produce literature that contains problems and issues that come with the "reimagining and reconstructing [of] the locations we study" (Parks 73). Transnational literature is therefore in its essence transcultural literature. In our Asian experience, transcultural literature's creation may be said to result from the post-colonial experience of most national literary fields in Asia that had direct experience of being transgressed and dominated by some outside power.

Another thing that must be emphasized, and this may be perceived as one of the ills of a global literature, is that global literary taste is being moved to sameness or universality. One notices the paradox that as entities fight to be individuated, the more similar they become. As individuals from around the globe become exposed to diverse cultures, a unifying "global taste" is becoming more evident.

An example of this global "literary taste" is the increasing similarity of what works are contained in the bestseller lists around the world. A big reason why such a similarity in popular reading taste is possible in a multilingual world is the growing importance and dependence of the literary field on the literary art and later, industry of translation.

The importance of being translated into English

Today, the most important language to be translated into is English. As linguist, David Crystal argued in his book *English as a Global Language:* "... a quarter of the world's population is already fluent or competent in English and this figure is steadily growing... No other language can match this growth" (Crystal 6)

With all the capital the English language has in the literary field of the world, or what is now referred to as the field of global literature, the works of non-Anglophone writers in their native languages need to be translated into the English language for these works to gain literary prominence or distinction.

The age of globalization has created a niche for the practice of translation to become an industry and this industry is naturally linked to publishing houses (and their associated literary workers) which in this age have also become international conglomerates whose center is traceable to the English-speaking United States, the biggest proponent of the economic and cultural globalization movements.

Characteristics of global literature

The editors of the online literary magazine, *n+1* sought to describe what globalization means in terms of literature. Global Literature is said to possess the following characteristics: first, it reflects the global flow of currency and consumption, thus it reflects global capitalism; second, it tends to accept as a given the tastes of an international middlebrow audience; and third, it is "defined more by a set of institutions than a convergence of projects." To expand the last description, the most important institution today, according to the editors of *n+1* magazine, is the university. Universities have become centers that stimulate readers of fiction to accept cultural diversity through the introduction by its cultural workers, the educators, of peripheral writers in their class syllabi. Thus, through the aid of class syllabi, some unknown fictional works have entered the domain of the canonical, which has recently become diverse in content. It must also be noted that many of the contemporary writers who produce global literature are university appointees (teachers, researchers, or fellows) who have gone to renowned universities for diverse reasons such as political exile, cultural exchange, and so on. In short, these writers have also a myriad of transnational experiences.

Teaching global literature in our classrooms

The problem that may emanate with global literary texts is that a sloppy handling of such texts in our classroom may result in the erasure of the uniqueness of the text, which includes its cultural ethnicity. This situation is more apparent when the literary work for consideration comes from a social reality far removed from the reality of its readers. To combat this possibility, we who teach literature must consciously carry out our role as *cultural researchers* as we guide our students to discovering the hidden gems of our predominantly translated, global literary texts. As Lawrence Venuti puts it: "[r]eading a work in translation is reading in a '*double focus*,' encompassing not just the foreign text and culture, but the text and culture of the translation" (Venuti 93).

It is a necessity then to lead the students to come up with multiple readings of the literary texts as we dissect the texts by reading behind and around them, even reading them interconnectedly with other texts we have come across in our classroom. That is to say, a formalist, close-reading of a text may not be sufficient when engaging with a global text, especially a translated, global text which has been re-contextualized for its readers.

Perhaps one thing that we can make visible in our classrooms as we engage in translated global literary texts is the reality that we are reading works that are translated. It has been widespread practice for educators not to focus on or even mention that the literary work for study is a translated work. Perhaps it is because we believe that a close-reading of a work in a literary classroom is enough. Now, in this new global literary context, it may be necessary to have a healthy dose of *suspicion* as we read translated works. Why the need for suspicion?

Language is a fragile thing whose meaning is easy to misconstrue. Translation which is never a perfect rendition of the original work must be contextualized. We should start asking the following questions in our classroom more frequently: is this literary work translated? Who translated it? When was it translated and for whom is this translation made? Answers to such questions alongside our background research on the text would provide a better grasp of the cultural features found in the texts that would otherwise be ignored or forgotten. Moreover, this multi-level reading of reading behind, around, and interconnectedly would also urge our students to reflect on their cultural reality as they wrestle with the translated literary work.

A sampling of three Asian-global writers

The second half of this paper focuses on three Asian writers whose novels are now being widely circulated in the global literary field. It must be noted that worldwide, since the eighteenth century, the novel, (replacing poetry and drama), has become the most popular literary form. This might be perhaps because it most closely represents the lives of most people. The novel became increasingly popular as its social scope expanded to include characters and stories about the middle and working classes. Because of its readership, which included a significant percentage of women and the middle class, the novel became the form which most addressed the domestic and social concerns of these groups.

The three writers whose works I will discuss are first, the widely popular Japanese writer Murakami Haruki; second, the South Korean Kim Young-ha, whose works are gaining prominence globally; and third is the global "newbie," Philippine writer, FH Batacan. This section does not attempt to provide thorough analyses of these writers' texts, but only provide an overview of their works' features, particularly, their global features, which I propose to be unlocked through a multilayered reading in our classrooms.

Murakami Haruki and *1Q84*

Murakami's case fits the definition of transculturation in literature. Murakami is the most significant contemporary author who has opened up contemporary Japanese literature to a global readership. His texts are often described to be borderless, and this has been a boon and a bane because in such a description lie the accusations that his texts are non-committal and culturally scentless. However, upon closer inspection, it can be argued that Murakami's texts do still in fact capture the eclectic spirit and ennui of Tokyo and other urban centers in Asia. However, these interests are secondary to his interest of presenting his texts as "global" first. By this I mean that Murakami consciously wants his texts to address global concerns first, then address issues that are of national interest. But when one thinks about global interests, doesn't one also take in national interests in the process? Thus, Murakami's literary interests are fluid between national and the global. He writes about Japan for the Japanese after the Second World War, the Japan that experienced an economic miracle, and the Japan that has lost its "soul" and is now seriously searching for it. And he also writes for the world when he addresses issues like terrorism, religious fanaticism, the changing role of the citizen, etc. Murakami's borderlessness places him in the growing field of transnational or global literature—literature that is at once different and familiar.

From the conception of the novel *1Q84* (trans. 2011), Murakami wanted to create a novel comparable to those written by world-renowned, canonized writers, particularly that of Fyodor Dostoyevsky. The work was consciously written to be a novel with the value of a legacy. It is a very self-conscious novel in a postmodern sense. This characteristic might be its biggest weakness. Yet, this weakness may be overlooked when one reflects on what the novel is able to portray. *1Q84* is a novel that draws on Japan's individual and collective history from the Second World War to the present 21st century, and because of this achievement, Murakami was able to achieve what he sought to do: a comprehensive novel in the tradition of Dostoevsky. The plot is painfully and cleverly constructed to be multilayered, metafictive in style, and historically grounded.

The work is translated by two longtime translators of Murakami, Harvard professor Jay Rubin, and University of Arizona professor, Philip Gabriel. Both translators are Americans who work closely with Murakami in the process of translating his works.

1Q84 addresses the following themes: love in the postmodern time, the postcolonial baggage of Japan as a former imperial nation, patriarchy and women's fight for equality, the issues surrounding the publishing world, the persistence of traditional beliefs in modern Japan, the role of religion in a postmodern society, and the presence of society's dark side. These real social issues are addressed by the novel using a plot that moves from realist fiction to the fantastic.

Kim Young-ha and *Your Republic Is Calling You*

Kim Young Ha's writing reflects the turbulence in the Korean literary field. This field is becoming increasingly global along with the city of Seoul where most of Kim's novels are set. It would be truly difficult for a writer to write out of his historical context. In Kim's case, he chronicles his historical period by focusing on the transformations inside his definitive characters.

According to critic, Younju Ryu (as reported in Tseng 2007), Kim's literary landscape is a familiar one to Western readers. It is a world of detached, city dwellers with blasé voices that are transnational in their social positions as well as in their consumption of Western and Eastern products. With such characters, Kim creates multilayered worlds where reality and fantasy blur. One does not speak of "a reality" in Kim's works but of "different levels of reality."

The second novel by Kim that was translated into English is his *Empire of Light* which has been re-translated to *Your Republic is Calling You* in 2010. The translation is by Korean-American Kim Chi-Young.

This novel is being sold as a spy novel because of the obvious reason that its central character, Ki-yong, was a North Korean spy dispatched to the South some 21 years back. In the decades in the South he carved a life for himself as a "regular Joe," an average employee with a family. In 24 hours, Ki-yong has to make a decision to go back to the North or to confess his espionage to the authorities in the South and face the consequences. This decision must be made as demanded by the cryptic e-mail he received in the morning which, decoded, was an Order 4, a command to go back to the North.

Although *Your Republic is Calling You* is set in South Korea, it is one of the very few works I have come across that gives the atmosphere of living in North Korea via the introspection of Ki-yong. For instance, in the chapter called "12:00 pm: Harmonica Apartments," Ki-yong recalled his childhood in a completely different Korea where hardships not only physical and mental, but most especially, emotional, were the daily fare. The young Ki-yong lost his mother through a suicide caused by depression which had no hope of being addressed in the North where it was not perceived as something curable. Another section in the novel that catches one's attention is the section called "1:00 p.m. The Hilton Hotel in Pyongyang." Here it is detailed how the best students, those selected to be spies to the South, were prepared to blend in culturally and socially after they were dispatched. The place they trained in was a re-creation, a "little Seoul," filled with individuals who dressed as South Koreans. The "local people" were either kidnapped from the South or came to the north voluntarily. Ki-yong reflects on that incident in his life and reaches the conclusion that the North with its very different ideology even fumbled in re-creating a Seoul for its would-be-spies. He recalls the stereotypes manifested there, perhaps because the training camp really had a theatrical feel to it—perhaps he thought the entirety of North Korea was a theater: "Like actors on set, North Koreans went about their days, conscious of the eyes of the "director" and "cast" (Kim 124).

The action in this novel is both external and internal. Characters are well-rounded, and it leaves one with a string of questions about human interaction and the role of the nation in developing its people. Yes, it does ask tough questions. Even more, it challenges us, especially us Asians, to confront the reality of North Korea and at least to attempt to see the perspective of the thousands who call North Korea their republic.

FH Batacan and *Smaller and Smaller Circles*

The first book of Filipina, FH Batacan (pen name of Maria Felisa H. Batacan), *Smaller and Smaller Circles*, while written originally in English, may still be easily classified as global literature. First, in the Philippine literary field, Batacan's novel is among the few to utilize the crime/thriller genre. Before this novel, Philippine fiction widely made use of the mainstream genre of realism. Batacan's successful fusion of the Western genre of crime fiction with a plot that is unmistakably Filipino has created a triumph for Philippine literature of the 21st century. As a result, local writers have begun to experiment with the crime genre to speak of their reality. As proof of how successful Batacan's first book is, she received three of the most prestigious local awards for it: the Palanca Grand Prize in 1999, the Manila Critics Circle's National Book Award in 2002, and the Madrigal Gonzalez Award in 2003. In a country like the Philippines, where it is uncommon for locally published books to be reprinted after the initial 1,000 copies of the book are printed, Batacan's book was reprinted four times[1].

The other reason that makes this novel part of the growing set of texts classified as global literature is due to its being taken in by an international publisher, Soho Press, for international release. According to Rudy Martinez, Soho Press's marketing manager, Soho took over the license of the novel after the ten-year UP Press license expired. Soho's associate publisher, Juliet Grames, saw the potential of the novel, and asked Batacan if she was willing to expand the novel, especially the priest's character, for the novel to be more attuned to the format of global crime fiction. After some revisions, Batacan's expanded novel was re-released for an international market in 2015. Moreover, Ruel de Vera of *Philippine Daily Inquirer* reported that an independent Filipino producer would be adapting the novel to film, slated to be shown in 2017, much to the delight of Batacan's growing readership. It is also said that Batacan is currently busy writing a prequel for the novel, tentatively titled *The Weight of Sin,* also for international release[2].

So, what is Batacan's influential novel about? The novel begins with a mutilated child's corpse, with the face, heart, and genitalia gone, discovered in the Philippines's biggest garbage dump in Metro Manila, Payatas. The discovery is horrific, and yet, the setting also contributes to the attack on the reader's sensibilities. Payatas is where the poorest of the poor have relocated. There they eke out a living by rummaging through sellable rejects in the mountains of trash. The children who discover the corpse tell their local priest, Fr. Emil, about what they found.

---

1 Batacan now joins the still elite rank of novelists such as Nick Joaquin, Lualhati Bautista, Eric Gamalinda and Carla Pacis whose literary works have been reprinted. Many thanks to Prof. Ramon Sunico of the Department of English, Ateneo de Manila for this short list.

2 This information was announced in a book-signing event in Manila where Batacan read a sample from this new work. The blogger behind Bookmarked! covered this event.

The unlikely "detectives" who will solve the crime are Fr. Augusto "Gus" Saenz, SJ, a forensic anthropologist and methodical detective, and Fr. Jerome Lucero, a clinical psychiatrist. These Jesuits are described as having been schooled in top Ivy League schools in the West. They also teach in a local university (whose description is clearly that of Ateneo de Manila). Their tastes and sensibilities are clearly bourgeois. Both of them come from well-to-do families and yet their religious training and spiritual nature balance their view of their nation and keep them close to the poor. Fr. Emil seeks their help in solving the crime since the police have no clear leads to a suspect.

Clearly, with Batacan's use of the crime fiction/ thriller as a genre, the literary work is allowed a certain flexibility in exposing the roots of the ills of society. The ability of supposed outsiders to the judicial process of the country (the priests) to step into the center of social events and help restore equilibrium to the system is indicative of the failure of the system to govern or hold things together. *Smaller and Smaller Circles* exposes the weakness of the Philippine bureaucracy and justice system in solving a crime in a highly accessible and contained site, the Payatas dumpsite. This work would leave us and its audience to reflect on the failure of our governing systems, which reverberate back to the failure of their colonial predecessors.

Concluding thoughts

It is comforting to know that more and more Asian writers are penetrating the global scene and that their works are rightfully being classified as global literature. As teachers and researchers our goal is to help our audience, our students or readers, to better engage with this growing body of works by encouraging them to read actively the texts with the knowledge that these works have had modifications either through translation from source language to target language or by editorial modifications as dictated by the taste that emerges from the global literary field.

Still, as much as we celebrate the export of Asian novels to the global stream, we should still cultivate a healthy suspicion in reading these translated works so as not to remove the ethnicity or cultural scent of each work. Truly, in the age of global literature, the struggle to maintain the identity of the text is a necessary struggle that we agents of literature must continue to wage.

References

Batacan, F. H. (2002). *Smaller and smaller circles.* Quezon City: University of the Philippines Press.

Crystal, D. (2003) *English as a global language* (2nd ed). Cambridge: Cambridge University Press.

Editors. (2013). World Lite: What is Global Literature? *n+1 magazine*. nplusonemag.com.

Jay, P. (2010). *Global matters: The transnational turn in literary studies.* Ithaca: Cornell University Press.

Kim, Y. (2010). *Your republic is calling you.* Chi Young-Kim, tr. Boston: Mariner Books.

Martinez, R. (2015). The story behind: FH Batacan's *Smaller and Smaller Circles.* sohopress.com.

Murakami, H. (2011). *1Q84*. Jay Rubin and Philip Gabriel, tr. New York: Alfred A. Knopf.

Parks, T. (2011). The Nobel individual and the paradoxes of 'international literature. *The Times Literary Supplement.*

"Smaller and Smaller Circles," *Bookmarked!*, 12 Jun 2016.

Tseng, A. (2007). Discovering Kim Young-ha. UCLA Center for Near Eastern Studies. international.ucla.edu.

Venuti, L, ed. (2012). *The Translation Studies Reader* (3rd ed). London: Routledge.

*

Bienvenido F. Nebres, S.J.

Education for a Globalizing Asia

Balancing Competitiveness and Relevance

THE TITLE OF THIS TALK is "Education for a Globalizing Asia: Balancing Competitiveness and Relevance." "Competitiveness" addresses what the call for papers for this conference says are the beneficial effects of internationalization, while the "relevance" part addresses some of its detrimental effects on educational development cited by other observers.

Addressing competitiveness

When we talk about *internationalization* in our Asian universities, our major concern is continuing growth in excellence, especially academic and research excellence, and competitiveness among ourselves and with the world. I have dedicated much of my life to developing mathematics and science in the Philippines and I have worked for over four decades with colleagues in East-Southeast Asia and the world in science and technology. Among the achievements I take greatest pride in is my contribution to building a vigorous community of mathematicians and other scientists, notably in physics and chemistry, from a very low starting point in the 1970s.

In the years I was president of the Ateneo de Manila University, I also dedicated much effort to help our university engage the new world of internationalization, university rankings, research excellence, competitiveness, and benchmarking.

In my work in science and mathematics dating from 1972, I helped develop extensive linkages with fellow mathematicians and scientists in Southeast Asia, as well as with those from Japan, Australia, and France. This period, from the 1970s to the 1990s, was also a period of rapid development of universities in our region and the world, and there was a push towards competitiveness and higher levels of excellence.

One of the contributions I continue to try to make is to identify and nurture talent. I co-teach a course in mathematics problem-solving (doing really difficult problems) during our summer sessions. This past summer I had one of my best classes ever and I was truly impressed by their talent and hard work. The mathematics community was also so delighted that we finally won not just one but two golds in the International Mathematics Olympiad, moving from 36th to 17th place—ahead of France, according to a French mathematician friend.

The challenge of relevance

Many years ago, a Japanese friend told me something I have never forgotten: "A country can only move as fast as its slower members."

A few days ago, I was in a satellite high school that we helped build in a poor village in Nueva Ecija. I met with the teachers and pupils and, sadly, they had no math textbooks nor any other math teaching materials for Grades 7-9. For the past 20-30 years, the average performance in the National Achievement Tests in second year and fourth-year high school for the Philippines has been 40-45%.

Turning from competitiveness to relevance, the question for me is, "So we are all working very hard to achieve competitiveness and excellence, following America and Western Europe, but are we working as hard and making real progress on the education needs of our slower members?" For the Philippines, the answer sadly is NO.

Competitiveness reference point is America

I would like to connect this challenge with the main part of the title: "Educating for a Globalizing Asia." When we speak of globalization or internationalization, our reference point is almost always North America and the UK or the English-speaking countries.

Many decades ago, someone said, "Japan makes television sets so people can see America." Similarly today, when we talk about the internet and connectivity, benchmarks, research journals, literature reviews, most of what we see is the United States.

The US is great for the faster members of society. For example, in the last International Mathematics Olympiad, the US team was number one, but the names of the team members were: Ankar Bhattarchaya, Michael Kural, Allen Liu, Junyao Peng, Ashwin Sah—all Asians, all very talented and given the needed support and nurture in the US to be number one.

I am myself a beneficiary of this part of American academic culture. Since I was in a seminary for the priesthood during my high school and college days, I did not have a mathematics undergraduate degree and had taken very few formal mathematics courses. I explained in my college application that I had studied most of the mathematics by myself. Stanford and a couple of other top US universities accepted me without the usual academic formalities.

Conclusion: Internationalization following North American standards is most likely the right thing for the faster members of our Asian societies.

US is not the right model for relevance

But then we turn to the question of relevance, which is "what are we doing for the slower members of our societies?" Here, the US may not be the right model. In a special issue for September 2016, *Scientific American* looks at the major challenges to our world concerning the future. One of them is "the threat of inequality," and the article basically says that it does not see equality improving in the US. In fact, the article says it is likely to grow worse. So on relevance as taking care of the slower members of our societies, the US is not the place to look. Where then should we look? In the field of elementary and high school education, where inequality probably does the greatest damage, I suggest we learn from each other in Asia.

For example, I have worked for several decades in the area of mathematics education. I have pointed out in several articles that the Philippines has gone through many mathematics education reforms: The New Math in the 1960s, Back to Basics in the 1970s, most recently the shift to the K to 12 system in elementary and high school. The pattern of reform is the same: The Department of Education begins with changing what is called the *Intended Curriculum.* This follows the pattern of the US where improving mathematics education is always based on coming out with new standards and new curricula.

These reforms are usually funded by a loan from the World Bank and they bring in experts from the US or Australia. These experts propose a reform of the intended curriculum, write new textbooks, etc. Given the 5-year framework for World Bank loans, they then rush the teacher training in the last couple of years. Several years later we find there has been no improvement. So we work again with the World Bank to reform the intended curriculum. We follow the same pattern and hope that finally this reform will work.

Of course, we eventually find that it does not. So we keep following the same pattern and keep hoping that the next time the results will be better. But after almost 50 years, the results have not improved.

If instead of looking to the US or Australia, we looked to our neighbors, say Japan, we would find a very different process of educational reform. I have written in a couple of articles noting that Japan works on a 12-year curricular change cycle. When they implement a new curriculum and new textbooks, they, at the same time, begin to gather feedback from classrooms, teachers, and schools, and over a period of time, consolidate the feedback at district, provincial, and eventually, national levels. This feedback from *actual classroom experience, from the implemented curriculum,* becomes an important component for the next curricular and textbook reform. It is an *empirical process,* like any good scientific process should be. It is also an *evolutionary process* of improvement, learning from what works or does not work and basing reform on the feedback from the classroom.

A second Asian example: If you follow news on international comparative education, you would have noticed a BBC headline story* in 2015, which read, "*Vietnam's performance in the last international PISA tests was a stunning achievement.*" (The Programme in International Student Achievement or PISA is the most important international comparative test at the high school level. It was originally only for the OECD countries, but others have adopted it since.)

The BBC article says:

> Participating in the tests for the first time in 2012, the country's 15-year-olds scored higher in reading, maths, and science than many developed countries, including the United States and the United Kingdom.
>
> It was an achievement that was as much of a surprise for Vietnamese officials as for outside observers.
>
> So how did Vietnam do so well?
>
> There are three key factors that contributed to these impressive results: committed leadership, a focused curriculum, and investment in teachers.
>
> People at the highest levels of government in Vietnam are thinking about the challenges they face in educating their young. Very few other countries have shown a similar level of forward thinking and determination.
>
> The nation's educators have also designed a curriculum that focuses on pupils gaining a deep understanding of core concepts and mastery of core skills.
>
> Contrast that with the mile-wide but inch-deep curriculums that you find in much of Europe and North America and you understand why so many of these Vietnamese students excel.

By the way, in the 2015 PISA tests, Vietnam did even better.

Committed leadership, a focused curriculum, and investment in teachers

A study commissioned by the Department of Education and done by Ateneo in the early 1990s asked: "What differentiates a low-performing from a high performing elementary school, given the same socio-economic environment?" Ateneo researchers in social psychology did a massive statistical study and came out with two differentiating variables:

The leadership of the principal and the support of the community.

The Ateneo Center for Educational Development (ACED) and Synergeia Foundation have followed this guide, engaging the leadership of mayors, barangay captains, principals, and the support of the community, the teachers, parents, and civic organizations. We have seen great improvement in the towns where the mayors exert leadership, an approach similar to what Vietnam says has been central to their success.

So, for the challenge of relevance, I suggest we revise the statement in this conference's preliminary statement, which says: "The implementation of policies geared towards internationalizing schools following North American and Western European standards have become more urgent," to take into account the possibility that while this may well work for the faster members of our societies, we can learn more from our own neighbors when it comes to providing better education for the great majority, the slower members of our societies.

If we do this, we also need to address another challenge, that of research publication. In my own experience in international mathematics education, a paper which says that the usual pattern of school improvement based on a new intended curriculum is not effective, and a better mode is the classroom feedback system in Japan and engaging the leadership of the mayor and the principal, *will not find easy publication in Western journals*. This happens because it does not fit into Western models and theories of educational reform. I have expressed these concerns in several international meetings.

My colleagues from Japan and Southeast Asia were sympathetic, but my colleagues from the West were not. So we have to work to publish our own research journals.

Parenthetically, we also need to revise our rules regarding surveys of the literature, because the vast majority of the literature will be from the West and we might never shift our gaze to our own neighbors.

In an article written for a *Festschrift* in my honor in 2011, my longtime colleague and friend, Prof. Lee Peng Yee of Singapore, wrote that in various international talks I have given, most recently, an invited address at the Centennial of the International Commission on Mathematical Instruction in Rome in 2008, I said: "Over four decades of such mathematics education reform in the Philippines, we have experienced a series of interventions from these approaches. So far, the approaches Western experts introduced from their own experience have not worked."

Once again: if we wish to address seriously the challenge of relevance, meaning, *taking care of the slower members of our societies,* then we need to shift our gaze from the US and the West and find effective ways to work and learn from each other. We also need to develop our own journals to publish our research findings.

*

Danilo A. Arao

Globalization, Deregulation, and Quality of Education in the Philippines*

AN ANALYSIS of the state of education in the country leads one to ask why age-old problems persist despite government initiatives to study the situation and formulate certain policy reforms. We can only analyze our educational system by looking at the roots of its problems and determining for whose interests it is being maintained.

Education can either be an instrument of liberation or subjugation (see Freire 1984; Postman and Weingartner 1969). It can promote either "popular culture" characterized by obedience and conformity or "counter-culture" characterized by resistance and change. We need not stress our pivotal role as teachers in the formal educational system. We are all engaged in a profession whose main prerequisites are our intellectual acumen and our commitment to serve. And contrary to popular belief,

---

* This paper is an expanded and updated version of my article titled "Deregulation at the Expense of Quality Education" in the book, *Mula Tore Patungong Palengke: Neoliberal Education in the Philippines*, edited by Lumbera, Guillermo, and Alamon, and published by IBON Books in 2007. Since there is no qualitative change in the policy direction of past and present administrations, the major arguments in this paper remain valid even if the benefit of hindsight gives me the opportunity to further explain them.

our role goes *beyond* teaching, since we are also engaged in research and extension work.

Our passion for sharing knowledge and molding young minds drives us to do what we are doing now. Our inherent hunger for information and insatiable desire to read allow us to continuously teach the same disciplines and topics year after year, using different approaches and enriching the content. Indeed, we continue to learn so that we can teach, and we continue to teach so that we can learn. There are objective and subjective forces for such passion, desire, and hunger among us.

Objectively speaking, we are all raised in a society that looks upon learned individuals as the hope of the country. Consequently, our parents or guardians inculcate in us the value of education at a time of poverty and deprivation. We are taught that education is an intellectual investment, something that we can use in the future to ensure a good and comfortable life. What our parents or guardians say are complemented by the reality of poverty that we see around us, from a neighbor who constantly borrows money from practically everyone, to our own teacher who sells tamarind in class to augment his or her income. (Even at a young age, we already become aware of the social class we belong to and of the need to change our lives for the better.)

At a subjective level, our personal ambitions to graduate and get a good paying job are replaced by a commitment to serve the people, particularly those who are marginalized. This, however, is not necessarily a whimsical decision but rather a product of deep appreciation of the prevailing social reality. Our class consciousness is further deepened not only by what our professors taught us but also by our involvement in organizations and the prodding of our classmates and friends. We see the convergence of both theory and practice in analyzing what is happening around us and in realizing the need to act and contend.

Indeed, there is material basis for our continuing commitment to teaching. Notwithstanding the problems facing the country's educational system right now, we perform our respective jobs and, at the same time, fight for our rights and welfare.

Unlearning environment

Our resolve to do what is right does not falter even with the sorry state of our educational system. That education has become inaccessible to many may be gleaned from official statistics. As of School Year (SY) 2012-2013, data from the Department of Education (DepEd) show that the completion rate was pegged at 73.67% at the elementary level and 74.81% at the secondary or high school level (see Table 1). This simply means that out of 10 pupils, only seven can finish elementary education. And out of the seven, only five students can finish secondary education. In other words, only half of those at the elementary level can graduate from high school.

This is the case even if 18.98 million students (or 87.77% of total enrolled elementary and high school students) go to public schools. Aside from the fact that elementary and secondary public schools account for 78.28% of total schools in the country, the highest law of the land explicitly states that the State shall provide for "a system of free public education in the elementary and high school levels" ("The 1987 Constitution", 1987: 51).

Nothing much has changed in the past 10 years. I wrote in my 2007 paper that then Education Secretary Jesli Lapus disclosed that for every 100 pupils who enter Grade 1, only 66 reach Grade 6, 58 reach first year high school, 23 reach the first year in college, and 14 can earn a college degree. Lapus explained that there are 200,000 six-year-old children (accounting for 8% of the age group's population) who are deprived of formal education. He said that out of 2.6 million children who enter Grade 1, more than 800,000 fail to finish Grade 6 (Arao 2007: 46).

Access to education becomes worse upon reaching the tertiary level, since a little more than 20% of the school age population of 16-21 years old can manage to enroll. To make matters worse, only 68.36% of them can reach fourth year college (Arao 2007: 47). Latest data show that private tertiary schools outnumber public tertiary schools. In SY 2012-2013, there were only 667 public schools throughout the country, as opposed to 1,652 private ones. It should not be a surprise therefore that there are around 1.9 million students in private tertiary schools as against 1.4 million enrollees in public tertiary schools (see Table 2).

Table 1

Selected basic education Data (School Year 2012-2013)

	Elementary	Secondary	Total
Schools	46,404	12,878	59,282
Public	38,659	7,748	46,407
Private	7,745	5,130	12,875
Enrolment	14,509,690	7,110,944	21,620,634
Public (DepEd)	13,259,489	5,641,898	18,901,387
Public (SUC)	13,836	60,699	74,535
Private	1,236,365	1,408,347	2,644,712
Public School Teachers (not including laboratory schools of SUCs but includes SPED teachers and teachers for Kinder)	377,831	169,743	547,574
Participation Rate or Net Enrolment Rate from primary (Grade IV) to Intermediate (Grade V)	95.24%	64.61%	
Completion Rate	73.67%	74.81%	
Dropout Rate or School Leavers (SY 2011-2012)	6.38%	7.82%	
Achievement Rate (as of SY 2011-2012)	66.79%	48.90%	
Mathematics	66.47%	46.37%	
Science	66.11%	40.53%	
English	66.27%	51.80%	
Hekasi (Geography/History/Civics)	65.97%	51.27%	
Filipino	69.15%	54.22%	
Gross Teacher-Student Ratio	1:36	1:35	

Source: Department of Education, 2013

Just the same, there was a substantial increase in the number of public tertiary school enrolees. Compared to 829,181 public school enrolees in Academic Year (AY) 2003-2004 (Arao 2007: 47), the figure increased by 71.62% to 1,423,004 in AY 2012-2013 (see Table 2). That the parents or guardians cannot sustain the high cost of education of their children may be rooted in the situation of low wages amidst high cost of living. Indeed, there is a need to distinguish between *free education* and *free tuition.* Government may have been able to provide for the latter at the elementary and high school levels but parents or guardians still shoulder the daily expenses of children going to school.

Table 2

Selected Higher Education Data (School Year 2012-2013)

Schools	2,319
Public (with satellites)	667
Private	1,652
Enrolment	3,317,530
Public	1,423,004
Private	1,894,526
Graduates	535,574
Public	229,425
Private	306,149
CHED Scholarship/Student Loan Grantees	1,280,876
Faculty Members	135,478
Public	49,366
Private	86,112
Performance (Percent Passing) in licensure examination	42.61%

Source: data.gov.ph, 2015

In December 2006, data from the National Wages and Productivity Commission (NWPC) showed that a family of six living in Metro Manila needed PHP768 to fulfill food and non-food requirements for one day. In areas outside Metro Manila, the required family living wage ranged from PHP478 (Eastern Visayas) to PHP1,008 (Autonomous Region in Muslim Mindanao). At that time, the minimum wage was not able to fulfill cost of living requirements. In Metro Manila, for example, the PHP350 daily minimum wage only translated to a monthly gross pay of PHP6,160, which constituted only 36.54% of the required family living wage amounting to PHP16,860 (Arao 2007: 46).

According to a 2001 NWPC study titled "Development of Methodology for Estimating the Living Wage," living wage refers to "the amount of family income needed to provide for the family's food and non-food expenditures with sufficient allowance for savings/investments for social security so as to enable the family to live and maintain a decent standard of human existence beyond mere subsistence level, taking into account all of the family's physiological, social and other needs" (as cited in Arao 2007: 46-47). The family living wage assumes that a Filipino family has an average of six members and that two of the family members (usually the mother and father) are earning.

Analyzing the latest daily minimum wage rates in the country's 16 regions, we notice that there is no substantial increase in wages through the years (see Table 3). The NCR's current daily minimum wage rate of PHP491 translates, for example, to a 40.28% increase over a 10-year period.

Table 3

Daily Minimum Wage Rates, Non-Agriculture (as of August 2016)*

	Daily Minimum Wage Rate (in ₱)
National Capital Region (NCR)	491.00
Cordillera Administrative Region (CAR)	285.00
Region I (Ilocos)	253.00
Region II (Cagayan Valley)	300.00
Region III (Central Luzon)	364.00
Region IV-A (CALABARZON)	378.00
Region IV-B (MIMAROPA)	285.00
Region V (Bicol)	265.00
Region VI (Western Visayas)	298.50
Region VII (Central Visayas)	353.00
Region VIII (Eastern Visayas)	260.00
Region IX (Western Mindanao)	280.00
Region X (Northern Mindanao)	318.00
Region XI (Southern Mindanao)	317.00
Region XII (Central Mindanao)	275.00
CARAGA (classified as Region XIII in NWPC data set)	275.00
Autonomous Region in Muslim Mindanao (ARMM)	265.00

Source: National Wages and Productivity Commission, 2016

**Note: For regions whose wage rates vary, the highest value is considered.*

At present, a public school teacher with the rank of Teacher 1 belongs to salary grade (SG) 11, earning a gross monthly salary of PHP19,077 (Manalansan 2016). Wherever he or she goes, however, this is still not enough to provide for the needs of a family with six members. The situation is even worse for a government employee who belongs to SG 1 since he or she only gets around PHP9,478 monthly (Department of Education 2016).

In the eyes of government, however, teachers and other workers do not need to struggle for higher wages since poverty is supposedly not a major problem in the country. If the government is to be believed, a person with only PHP51.88 can meet food and non-food requirements in one day (see Table 4).

Globalization of education

In studying the educational system in India, Azad (n.d.: 5) observed that "it is difficult to assess not only the nature and dimensions of globalization, but also what it might mean to the field of education." Nevertheless, it was stressed that "[a]ny thoughtless entry into the global educational market can end up in harming the vital interests of students for generations to come" (Azad n.d.: 12).

In the case of the Philippines, the root cause of the dismal state of the educational system is the development thrust of the government through the years. Adherence to globalization has become a bane to the development of our educational system along nationalist, scientific, and mass-oriented lines. Instead, the youth are given an education that is colonial, feudal, and elitist (see Villegas 2007).

The colonial character of our educational system may be gleaned from Act No. 74 (1901) which established the public school system in the country. At that time, emphasis was given on the use of English as the medium of instruction, and the teaching of the three Rs (reading, 'riting, 'rithmetic) was oriented toward the introduction of the American way of life and the inculcation that American culture is superior to ours. Subsequent policies related to education did not seek to alter this orientation (see Lumbera 2007).

Feudalism, on the other hand, is seen in the way our educational system is managed. Instead of promoting critical thinking among the youth, education is used as an income-generating measure by the capitalist-owners and

Table 4
Poverty in the Eye of Government (2012)

	Annual Per Capita Poverty Threshold (₱)	Daily Per Capita Poverty Threshold (₱) a/ *	Poverty Incidence Among Families (%)
Philippines	18,935	51.88	19.7
National Capital Region (NCR)	20,344	55.74	2.6
Cordillera Administrative Region (CAR)	19,483	53.38	17.5
Region I (Ilocos)	18,373	50.34	14.0
Region II (Cagayan Valley)	19,125	52.40	17.0
Region III (Central Luzon)	20,071	54.99	10.1
Region IV-A (CALABARZON)	19,137	52.43	8.3
Region IV-B (MIMAROPA)	17,292	47.38	23.6
Region V (Bicol)	18,257	50.02	32.3
Region VI (Western Visayas)	18,029	49.39	22.8
Region VII (Central Visayas)	18,767	51.42	25.7
Region VIII (Eastern Visayas)	18,076	49.52	37.4
Region IX (Western Mindanao)	18,054	49.46	33.7
Region X (Northern Mindanao)	19,335	52.97	32.8
Region XI (Southern Mindanao)	19,967	54.70	25.0
Region XII (Central Mindanao)	18,737	51.33	37.1
CARAGA	19,629	53.78	31.9
Autonomous Region in Muslim Mindanao (ARMM)	20,517	56.21	48.7

Source of basic data: Philippine Statistics Authority, n.d.
**a/ = annual per capita poverty threshold divided by 365*

an instrument of subjugation by the powers-that-be. The prevailing atmosphere in schools also has vestiges of feudalism. Generally speaking, the hiring and promotion of teachers, for example, rest not on qualification and performance but on how close they are to the administrators.

Elitism is manifested by the fact that education remains more of a privilege rather than a right. Notwithstanding the provision for free tuition in public elementary and high schools, school-related expenses remain prohibitive due to the high cost of living and the lack of government support. Education is also inaccessible especially in remote areas.

Manifestations of deregulation

An important tenet of globalization is deregulation. Gerston, Fraleigh, and Schwab (1988: 4) described deregulation as the "theme of the 1980s, referring to the de-emphasis of governmental oversight of activities in the private sector". Studying the economic history of the United States of America, they said,

> At a time when public functions have become increasingly intertwined with private functions, the deregulation movement has come to represent an effort at minimizing governmental impact on society, for the cost of regulation has been great in both dollars and manpower. (Gerston, Fraleigh, and Schwab 1988: 4)

In other words, deregulation refers to the removal of the regulatory environment of particular economic sectors. In a previous study on the downstream oil industry in 2005, I wrote that in the context of political economy, "an industry, composed of either private or public enterprises, is integrated into the market economy and provides a defined good or service to identified end-consumers. Theoretically, the determination of unit cost could either be profit-oriented or service-oriented" (as cited in Arao 2007: 50).

Adherence to globalization and its tenets (deregulation, liberalization, and privatization) results in the conversion of what used to be service-oriented sectors into profit-oriented ones. The current educational system proves to be no exception given the government's failure to provide quality education to the majority of the country's youth, as proven by the official statistics and policy pronouncements cited earlier.

Ironically, Art. XIV, Sec. 1 of The 1987 Constitution (1987: 51) states: "The State shall protect and promote the right of all citizens to quality education at all levels and shall take appropriate steps to make such education accessible to all."

Republic Act 7722 (Higher Education Act of 1994), which established the Commission on Higher Education (CHED), takes the issue of quality education one step further: "The State shall protect, foster, and promote the right of all citizens to *affordable quality education* at all levels and shall take appropriate steps to ensure that education shall be accessible to all" (Sec. 2, italics mine).

On the surface, agencies like the DepEd and the CHED are meant to regulate the country's educational system. Art. XIV, Sec. 4 (1) of The 1987 Constitution (1987: 52, italics mine), after all, requires regulation of the educational system: "The State recognizes the complementary roles of public and private institutions in the educational system and shall exercise *reasonable supervision and regulation* of all educational institutions."

While both DepEd and CHED provide a system of accreditation for all educational institutions, it cannot be denied that in the case of tertiary education, CHED policies prove the government's thrust towards "progressive deregulation" as early as 20 years ago. CHED Memorandum Order No. 46 (series of 1996) states that in order to provide more leeway for higher education institutions (HEIs) in determining curricular offerings and student eligibility requirements, "progressive deregulation vis-à-vis HEIs is hereby declared a policy of the Commission" (as cited in Arao 2007: 51). This particular order allows HEIs, subject to certain minimum requirements, to determine the eligibility of students who want to take up law, medicine, and dentistry. HEIs can also design the curricula of courses. Lastly, those that have Level III accreditation for Arts, Sciences, and three other professional courses are given the prerogative to offer new courses without the CHED's approval.

What has proven to be more detrimental to students, however, is the provision in Republic Act No. 8292 (1997), or the Higher Education Modernization Act of 1997, which states the following as among the powers of the boards of regents/trustees of state universities and colleges:

> *to fix the tuition fees and other necessary school charges*, such as but not limited to matriculation fees, graduation fees, and laboratory fees, as their respective boards may deem proper to impose after due consultations with the involved sectors.
>
> Such fees and charges, including government subsidies and other income generated by the university or college, shall constitute special trust funds and shall be deposited in any authorized government depository bank, and

> all interests [that] shall accrue therefrom shall [be] part of the same fund for the use of the university or college:
>
> Provided, That income derived from university hospitals shall be exclusively earmarked for the operating expenses of the hospitals.
>
> Any provision of existing laws, rules, and regulations to the contrary notwithstanding, any income generated by the university or college from tuition fees and other charges, as well as from the operation of auxiliary services and land grants, shall be *retained by the university or college*, and may be disbursed by the Board of Regents/Trustees for instruction, research, extension, or other programs/projects of the university or college: Provided, That all fiduciary fees shall be disbursed for the specific purposes for which they are collected.
>
> If, for reason of control, the university or college shall not be able to pursue any project for which funds have been appropriated and, allocated under its approved program of expenditures, the Board of Regents/Trustees may authorize the use of said funds for any reasonable purpose which, in its discretion, may be necessary and urgent for the attainment of the objectives and goals of the universities or colleges. (Sec. 4d, 3-4, emphasis mine)

This provision clearly empowers the SUC administrators to impose tuition increases to generate much-needed income. In the context of low budgetary allocation for education, the government, through the CHED, saw the need to deregulate tuition and other fees so that SUCs could become self-sufficient. This, of course, is done at the expense of impoverished students and parents whose incomes are not even enough to provide for the needs of their families.

Clearly, the deregulated regime is anathema to quality education.

Struggling against deregulation of education

It is in this context that we must analyze the kind of educational system that administrations past and present want to impose. It is in the interest of government to maintain docility instead of vigilance among the country's youth. They are, after all, the future labor force.

In the final analysis, the 2002 Basic Education Curriculum (BEC) and the 2016 K-12 program only seek to perpetuate a social order mainly characterized by blind obedience to the powers-that-be. It promotes a pedagogy that subjugates instead of liberates (see Freire 1984; Postman and Weingartner 1969).

The controversial integrated learning area has been euphemistically called MAKABAYAN (nationalist) in the past, but it is nothing but a hodge-podge of unrelated subjects geared toward, among others, reducing the number of textbooks and ensuring continued education even at a time of zero economic growth (i.e., which implies less budgetary allocation for education).

The Alliance of Concerned Teachers (ACT) has been consistent in its struggle for teachers' rights and welfare and quality education, and has provided a comprehensive critique of both the 2002 BEC and the K-12 program.

We do not need to repeat what has been argued before. We only need to remember that opposition to the 2002 BEC does not make us conservative critics or protectors of the status quo. The Medium-Term Higher Education Development and Investment Plan 2001-2004 (MTHEDIP), for example, is very explicit in the need to produce graduates who are globally competitive (Arao 2007: 52-53). While it also stresses the need to inculcate nationalism, it nevertheless promotes schemes that would allow increased private sector participation in tertiary education.

Given the domination of transnational corporations in our local economy, it becomes inevitable that foreign investors will further penetrate and influence the country's tertiary education especially with government approval. The MTHEDIP actually cites as a case study the partnerships of transnational corporations like IBM with, say, the Far Eastern University (FEU) in setting up the East-Asia College. The government also argues that we should "internationalize" our curriculum in order to attract as many foreign enrolees as possible as in the case of the Asian Institute of Management (AIM).

In order to further justify decreased budgetary allocation for education, the MTHEDIP advocates the commercialization and corporatization of the tertiary public school system. We need not argue at this point the negative repercussions these bring on teachers' rights and welfare, not to mention the content of the curriculum.

As we struggle for better working conditions of teachers, we also move toward attaining an educational system and culture that is nationalist, scientific, and mass-oriented. As Bauzon (1994: 162) argued, education should "be viewed as the true practice of freedom."

References

Arao, D. A. (2007). Deregulation at the expense of quality education. In B. Lumbera, R. Guillermo, & A. Alamon (Eds.), *Mula tore patungong palengke: Neoliberal education in the Philippines* (pp. 43-53). Quezon City: IBON Books.

Azad, J. L. (n.d..). Globalization and its impact on education: A challenge and an opportunity. Retrieved from https://www.scribd.com/doc/48392155/Globalization-and-Its-Impact-on-Education

Bauzon, P. T. (1994). *Fundamental philosophies of education.* Quezon City: National Book Store.

data.gov.ph. (2015, August 13). Higher education indicators for 2003-2013 [Data file]. Retrieved from http://data.gov.ph/catalogue/dataset/higher-education-institution/resource/77709bd9-2122-465b-88d9-4449e7257662

Department of Education. (2013, July 4). DepEd facts and figures [Data file]. Retrieved from http://www.deped.gov.ph/sites/default/files/datasets/2013/factsheetOct%20 25%202013.xls

Department of Education. (2016, March 10). DO 12, s. 2016 – Implementation of the first tranche compensation adjustment for civilian personnel, and military and uniformed personnel in the national government. Retrieved from http://www.deped.gov.ph/orders/do-12-s-2016

Freire, P. (1984). *Pedagogy of the oppressed.* New York: The Continuum Punlishing Corporation.

Gerston, L. N., Fraleigh, C., & Schwab, R. (1988). *The deregulated society.* California: Wadsworth, Inc.

Lumbera, B. (2007). Edukasyong kolonyal: Sanhi at bunga ng mahabang pagkaalipin. In B. Lumbera, R. Guillermo & A. Alamon (Eds.), *Mula tore patungong palengke: Neoliberal education in the Philippines* (pp. 1-7). Quezon City: IBON Books.

Manalansan, O. S. (2016, March 11). Teachers' salary increase table based on E.O. 201. *DepEd Forum.* Retrieved from http://depedforum.com/teachers-salary-increase-table-eo-201/

National Wages and Productivity Commission. (2016, August 3). Summary of current regional daily minimum wage rates: Non-agriculture, agriculture [Data file]. Retrieved from http://www.nwpc.dole.gov.ph/pages/statistics/stat_current_regional.html

Philippine Statistics Authority. (n.d.). Family income [Data file]. Retrieved from http://www.nscb.gov.ph/secstat/d_income.asp

Postman, N., & Weingartner, C. (1969). *Teaching as a subversive activity.* New York: Dell Publishing Co, Inc.

Republic Act 7722: Higher Education Act of 1994. 1993, July 26. Retrieved from http://ched.gov.ph/wp-content/uploads/2013/05/Republic-Act-7722.pdf

Republic Act No. 8292: Higher Education Modernization Act of 1997. 1997, June 6. Retrieved from http://www.ched.gov.ph/wp-content/uploads/2013/05/TRANSPARENCY-ABOUT-RA8292.pdf

The 1987 Constitution of the Republic of the Philippines. 1987. Mandaluyong City: National Book Store.

Villegas, E. M. (2007). Liberalism, neoliberalism and the rise of consumerist education. In B. Lumbera, R., Guillermo, & A. Alamon (Eds.), *Mula tore patungong palengke: Neoliberal education in the Philippines* (pp. 19-30). Quezon City: IBON Books.

*

Contributors

Dr. Theresa Alviar-Martin is assistant professor of curriculum and instruction at Kennesaw State University and formerly co-director of the Centre for Governance and Citizenship at the Education University of Hong Kong. Her research examines citizenship education in culturally diverse democracies from global and comparative perspectives. Alviar-Martin's writing has been published in several academic books and peer-reviewed journals, including *Teaching and Teacher Education*, *Journal of Educational Research*, *Teachers College Record*, and *Theory & Research in Social Education*.

Danilo A. Arao is associate professor of the Department of Journalism, College of Mass Communication, University of the Philippines (UP) Diliman. He is currently on study leave to write a dissertation on journalism and culture of impunity, as a requirement for the degree of Doctor philosophiae (Dr. phil.) at the Technische Universität Ilmenau in Germany.

Dr. Mark C. Baildon is associate professor and head of the Humanities and Social Studies Education Academic Group at the National Institute of Education (Singapore). His scholarly interests focus on ways to support social studies inquiry practices and 21st century literacies in new global contexts. He has published two books: *Social Studies as New Literacies in a Global Society: Relational Cosmopolitanism in the Classroom* (with James Damico, Routledge, 2011) and *Controversial History Education in Asian Contexts* (co-editor, Routledge, 2013).

Dr. Alona U. Guevarra is assistant professor at the Department of English, Ateneo de Manila University. She finished her graduate studies at the University of the Philippines Diliman. Her current research interests include environmental humanities, global literature, and the contemporary literatures of Japan and Korea.

Dr. Lukas S. Ispandriarno is senior lecturer at the Department of Communication Science, Faculty of Social Sciences at University of Atma

Jaya Yogyakarta. He is also head of the Master of Communication Science Program at the University of Atma Jaya Yogyakarta, Indonesia.

Dr. Martin Löffelholz is professor of Media Studies and director of the Institute of Media and Communication Science of Technische Universität Ilmenau, Germany. Concurrently, he serves as visiting professor at both the Universitas Atma Jaya Yogyakarta in Indonesia and the Ateneo de Manila University in the Philippines. From 2012 to 2015, he was the rector of the Swiss German University in Jakarta, Indonesia.

Dr. Jozon A. Lorenzana is assistant professor in the Department of Communication, School of Social Sciences, Ateneo de Manila University. Dr. Lorenzana's critical ethnographic research covers interrelated themes of social relations, identity, morality, emotions, and media practices among Filipino middle classes, migrant groups, and queer people.

Fr. Bienvenido Nebres, SJ served as president of the Ateneo de Manila University for eighteen years (1993-2011). He did extensive work to develop science and mathematics in the Philippines and in Southeast Asia and was elected in 2011 as National Scientist by the National Academy of Science and Technology (NAST). He continues to work as professor of Mathematics at the Ateneo de Manila and is engaged in various programs to help overcome poverty in the Philippines: improving public education in over 400 public schools with the Ateneo Center for Educational Development (ACED) and in over 200 municipalities, particularly in the Autonomous Region of Muslim Mindanao, with Synergeia Foundation; building homes and communities for the poor with Gawad Kalinga; and supporting young people engaged in social enterprises for poor communities.

Dr. Nida P. Rodriguez served Notre Dame University in Cotabato City in different capacities; faculty in the Language and Humanities Dept, dean of the College of Arts and Sciences, and dean of the Graduate School. Prior to her retirement in June 2017, she was director of the University Research and Publications Center. Her research engagements and outputs were commissioned, institutional, academic and collaborative researches especially in educational management and mentoring.

Index